VEGETABLES ON YOUR BARBECUE

Maggie Black

MULBERRY EDITIONS

MULBERRY EDITIONS 1992

ISBN 0-572-01755-3
Copyright © 1992 W. Foulsham & Co. Ltd.

Printed in Great Britain by
Cox & Wyman Ltd., Reading

CONTENTS

TALKING OF BARBECUING

PREPARE AHEAD OF TIME

ON YOUR BARBECUE

Line illustrations by Elaine Hill

TALKING OF BARBECUING

WHY NOT BARBECUE?

'You can't barbecue, you're a *vegetarian*!'

'Why on earth not?' is your right response to this quite common statement. 'After all,' you can go on, 'at least two-thirds of *all* barbecue foods are from plants anyway. Breads and rolls, marinades, chutneys and pickles and desserts don't have even a sniff of meat or fish in them. Nor do most barbecue sauces and bastes, nor salads.

'But you need steaks or chops for barbecue grilling.'

'And what makes you think that vegetarians don't grill and eat solid foods like other people? Savoury bean or cheese burgers and nut cutlets are delicious cooked this way. So are vegetable kebabs and kofta. Vegetable stir-fries and curries are first-class when cooked on a barbecue grill; it's the way they are done in the East. Then there are all the tasty foil-baked vegetables like potatoes and onions, and fruits too, of course, such as rum-baked bananas. What's more, there's some super new equipment on the market, so that you can fry eggs and vegetables or sliced fruit on the barbecue just as you can on a cooker in the kitchen. Vegetarians can have a top-class barbecued meal, I promise you; and everyone else will enjoy it too.

'In fact, there are so many vegetarians around these days, that it's a good idea to have some barbecued vegetarian foods as well as meat and fish at *every* barbecue party. In that way, you can entertain all your friends together without worrying; you'll know that they will all be scrumptiously fed.'

'Sounds like a good idea.'

'It is. Try it and see. This book is full of tasty vegetarian recipes, specially designed for barbecue cooking. Your meat-eating friends can use all the same sauces and side dishes, which will save work. And remember that these vegetarian dishes are generally cheaper than meat ones, so you'll save cash too . . .'

'Sounds even better! Let's have a go!'

YOUR BARBECUE GEAR

Your equipment will be the same whether you aim to barbecue steaks or nutburgers. You will need a barbecue of some kind, small or large, simple or grand, fuel and equipment for handling the fire. Household and kitchen tools will meet most of your needs for cooking and serving equipment, but there are some items which you should get specially because they will make your barbecuing much easier and more fun. They are marked with an * in the checklists below.

Equipment for handling the fire and barbecue

Shovel
Whether you use wood chunks, lump charcoal or briquettes, you will need a stout shovel for putting fuel on any barbecue, except a gas-fired one, and for clearing up hot ash afterwards.

Tongs, poker
You will also need stout tongs for moving individual pieces of fuel and for spreading it all. Use a poker for flicking grey ash off the fire, but not for spreading the burning material.

Bellows
Using bellows to create an extra draught saves your lungs, and makes a better fire than blowing on it.

Protective gloves, cloths
NEVER touch any part of a hot barbecue or its cooking equipment with bare hands. Both hold the heat for a long time even when they look innocently cool.

Sand or old barbecue cinders
Use these for dousing the fire after cooking. Do not use water as it may damage your barbecue. (A small pile of sand is also an essential safety feature in case of fire.)

Cleaning materials
You will need a wire brush, your usual detergent and perhaps oven cleaner.

Cooking equipment

Gloves, aprons
If one or two people are doing all the cooking, they will certainly each need gloves when handling the hot equipment, and aprons to protect their clothes.

Foil, paper towels, cloths
You will need foil for several purposes, such as wrapping vegetables for baking and protecting skewer ends. Paper towels and cloths are needed for mopping up drips.

Sharp knives, long-handled fork, board
Although you will prepare and cut up vegetables and other foods ahead of time, you will still need knives, a fork and a chopping board for any last-minute splitting or slicing.

Toasting tongs*
You will need several pairs of tongs for turning food items over on the grill. Never use a fork; the food tends to break up or dry out. Wooden tongs are now available as well as metal ones.

Kebab and other long skewers*
Keep a plentiful supply of both wooden and thin metal skewers. Vegetarian 'meatballs' should be cooked on thin wooden skewers.

Double-sided grill, vegetable or meat 'net'*
A double-sided hinged grill which holds the food between two layers of mesh is almost essential for grilling soft or thin items

such as 'burgers' which may break up. A metal 'net' holds securely small food items such as sliced or cubed vegetables which would otherwise slip through the bars of the grill.

Barbecue griddle pan*

This is a new feature in barbecue equipment which is especially suited to vegetarian cooking. A barbecue griddle pan is a solid rustproof cast aluminium plate with a detachable handle, designed for frying as in a frying pan. Two pegs on the underside fit between the bars of the grill (broiler) to keep it still and steady. Its three shallow compartments let you fry eggs and two vegetables at the same time. Foods are easy to turn over or lift off, just with an ordinary flat kitchen spatula.

Barbecue grill tray*

Another new feature is a re-usable foil tray with a ribbed base which collects drippings and juices, preventing fire flare-ups. Slots let the charcoal smoke flavour the food. Ideal for holding foil-wrapped items and for grilling or frying small portions of food when the surface is lightly oiled.

Basting brushes or mops, jugs*

You will need a brush or mop for each special 'baste' you use, as well as one for melted butter or oil. A tube baster is not really practical, having no handle.

Spit and motor (battery or electric), drip-tray*

Although optional, most barbecues have a place where a spit can be inserted. The costlier ones come ready equipped with a spit, but not usually with a motor. Luxury barbecues may have an electric spit motor. A drip-tray is only essential for spit-roasting.

'Cook's Table', trays, saucepans and other containers, coverings

Put food items ready for barbecuing on a trestle table or trolley covered with a plastic cloth. Place foods on easy-clean trays. If necessary, keep soups, barbecue 'simmerers', etc. in heavy saucepans which will stand level on the grill. Do not risk using pans with plastic or metal handles. Put bastes and relishes in jugs and bowls. Label everything clearly. Cover all food items with a loose sheet of foil or plastic sheeting.

Seasonings and spices

Salt and freshly ground black pepper are 'musts', but you should also offer a choice of spices which suit the food being barbecued. For instance, some people like the tang of paprika or finely grated lemon rind on grilled foods.

Serving equipment

1. *Bar table, ice bucket, can and bottle openers*
Keep alcoholic and soft drinks on a table apart from the food
to disperse your guests.

2. *Serving table*
Arrange salads, breads and other ready-to-use foods on a
separate table away from the foods to be cooked.

3. *Freezer bags, cold packs*
Salads, cold relishes, butter and cream keep fresh and fly-free
in a freezer bag containing a frozen cold pack.

4. *Salad and fruit bowls, bread basket, cake covers*
Use sturdy containers and avoid glass bowls. Breads and rolls
look best in a basket rather than on a plate or board. Cover
salads and desserts with transparent cake covers if possible.

5. *Serving tools for salads, gâteaux etc.*
Use sturdy plastic tools, brightly coloured to prevent them
getting lost.

6. *Insulated food flasks, pitchers, jugs, sugar bowl*
Soups prepared in advance, sauces and hot coffee or tea can
be kept hot in labelled insulated containers. Pour sauces into
jugs for serving. Milk can be served from its own container,
but remember to provide a sugar bowl.

7. *Condiments, relishes*

8. *Kitchen paper, tea towels*

Diners' and clearing equipment

Cardboard plates, mugs

Paper napkins

Cutlery
Forks or spoons will be needed for some vegetable items and
for salads and desserts. Knives may be needed for spreading
butter or margarine on bread. Teaspoons may be required for
hot drinks.

Waste bags

Mosquito and fly sprays
Useful.

SAFETY FIRST

Barbecuing is completely safe provided you guard against a few obvious risks. Make sure that children, especially, know what the risks are.

Make sure the site is safe to use

1. Site any portable barbecue in the open air, cn a patio or verandah open to the air or under shelter near the doors of a garage wide open to the air. Burning charcoal gives off dangerous carbon monoxide fumes.

2. Make sure the barbecue is clear of overhanging trees and low dry bushes. Clear the area of dry leaves, grass or twigs and dispose periodically of barbecuing debris such as used cardboard plates, napkins and cloths.

3. Do not site the barbecue on slippery or cobbled ground or on a wooden or vinyl-covered floor. A level concrete or paved floor is best. The barbecue must stand steady and level.

4. A strong breeze or draught may re-kindle fuel and blow smoke and sparks into people's faces. Put up an adequate wind shield if needed.

5. Never move a lighted barbecue if you can help it. If you have to shift it, wear heavy gloves and make sure the wind is at your back.

Light the fire correctly

Never use petrol (gasoline), lighter fluid or any volatile fuel to get the fire started. Such fuels are not only dangerous, they make the food taste unpleasant. There are several safe and effective aids to igniting the fire which you can use (page 11).

Look out — it's HOT

1. Wear heavy oven-gloves to touch any part of a barbecue after the fire is lit and even after you think it has died down. In daylight, it is impossible to 'see' red-hot charcoal; it will

appear white and dusty, even while still giving off burning heat. The grill and firepan can also be almost red-hot without seeming it.

2. Do not equip your barbecue with plastic or metal-handled tools, pans or spoons; they may be too hot to hold or may even melt. Use long-handled tools where possible. Well-wetted wooden tongs and spoons are easy to handle and do not char readily.

3. Douse any small flare-ups from drips of fat with a sprinkling of water as soon as they occur. Use sand or old barbecue cinders to smother burning fat.

4. Prevention is better than cure, but keep a tube of burn salve handy in case of small stinging burns from sparks or from touching the barbecue.

FUEL AND FIRE

Most people use charcoal for barbecuing because it is easy to use and store, but if you have a supply of hardwood logs or plenty of really dry twigs and branches, you can use wood.

Wood
Softwoods such as cedar or birch can be used to get your wood fire going because they burn fast, but the resin they contain make them smoke heavily and create sparks and flare-ups, so they are not suitable for the main fire. Never use pine or eucalyptus; they make the food taste of cough-mixture.

Hardwoods such as oak, ash and beech are best for your main fire because they burn slowly and give off greater heat than softwoods. A few sprigs of an aromatic herb such as bay or juniper added to the fire will scent the air and food even more pleasantly than the 'bonfire' scent of hardwood; or you can buy a packet of wood-burning herbs chosen for the purpose.

Make sure that any firewood you use is quite dry and solid, not crumbling. A local timber yard may supply shavings, chips and small off-cuts. Otherwise use twigs and bark to start the fire, then add larger short branches. Pile up a big supply of fuel before you start; you will certainly need more than you think.

Charcoal

There are two types of charcoal: lump charcoal made from both softwoods and hardwoods and charcoal briquettes made from hardwoods such as beech or oak and sometimes coal waste. Lump charcoal lights easily and burns quite fast, but tends to flare and give off sparks more than briquettes. Briquettes consist of compressed charcoal made into equal-sized small blocks or nuggets. They are easier to arrange in a compact 'bed' than lumps and they burn slowly and evenly, giving off intense heat without smoke or flame, which is ideal for barbecuing.

It is cheaper to buy charcoal in bulk than in small bags. It is also more convenient provided you can keep it dry. Even slightly damp charcoal will create clouds of smoke without really getting well alight. If your charcoal is only slightly damp, you can try drying it off first with a hair-dryer — but it is more sensible to store it in a dry place all the time.

Firelighters

Lighting a charcoal fire is child's play using modern firelighters. There is no need to use dangerous 'starters' such as methylated spirit or lighter fuel or, worse, to sprinkle your charcoal with petrol (gasoline). If you possess one, use a portable electric fire-starter or gas blow-lamp; both are efficient. Otherwise, use either self-igniting charcoal briquettes or the commonplace solid block white firelighters which you can break up or crumble and scatter among your charcoal. They are also sold in the form of granules. Jellied alcohol is another choice.

Gas-fired barbecues which are lighted just by turning a knob are of course foolproof (unless you run out of bottled gas).

Building the fire

Wood or charcoal need bottom ventilation to get set alight. If your barbecue has air vents or dampers, open them. Cover a solid firepan with foil, which reflects heat upward, then with pebbly gravel which provides a little upward draught and mops up spilt grease; you can wash and re-use it. Use bellows rather than lung-power; it is more effective.

Now place in the firepan either a few balls of squashed newspaper and some wood chips (for wood fires) or a few pieces of broken-up solid block fire-lighter or a handful of granules and some charcoal fragments (for charcoal fires). Cover with a small pile of twigs or charcoal — not too much! Light the fire with a taper.

When you light your fire will depend on the type and size of barbecue you have, the fuel and the weather. Any charcoal takes longer to get going and burns more slowly on a cold or damp day. A charcoal fire for grilling (broiling) should be ready for use in 25–40 minutes, depending on the type of charcoal, how tightly it is packed and whether it gets a good bottom draught. Manufacturers of the larger covered kettle or wagon-style barbecues usually tell you in their instruction leaflets how long to allow for the fire to reach grilling heat. A gas-fired barbecue, which uses lava rock, is ready to use in about 5 minutes.

As soon as the fire has 'caught', spread out the charcoal in an even layer with long-handled tongs. Leave space at the sides of the firepan for extra fuel; always add fuel at the sides, not on top of the fire — that smothers the heat. Keep a supply of fuel warm right beside the barbecue, and add some to the fire when the level burns low; you can stack burning fuel from the sides onto the centre of the fire at this stage if you keep it in a level layer and put the new fuel at the sides.

If you will be cooking for some time, say 'kettle' or spit-roasting for a party, you will clearly need more fuel than for a quick family fry-up. For spit-roasting, spread fuel on one side of the firepan only, parallel with the spit, and put a drip-tray under the spit itself, to catch any greasy drips.

To judge whether the fire is hot enough to cook on, hold your hand over it, palm down, at your expected cooking level. If you can hold it there for 4 seconds before having to pull it away, the temperature is probably about right for spit-roasting. If you can only hold it there for 2 seconds, you can use the grill (broiler) rack. If you think that the fire is not ready but want to start cooking quickly, open dampers, flick off any white ash with a poker and give it a puff or two with bellows. Remember that in daylight it may not seem to be burning at all; only the film of white ash will tell you.

To cool the fire a little, raise the rack an inch or two or move the food to the side of the fire where it is cooler.

Dousing the fire

Put out the fire as soon as cooking is finished if possible, to save fuel; you can re-use solid wood chunks or coals. Do not use water. It may damage a hot metal or brick barbecue and the wet fuel will take a long time to dry. Shovel the burning fuel into a bucket or a metal wheelbarrow and smother it with old barbecue cinders. Next day, riddle it to sift out the ash.

PLANNING A PARTY

The chief pleasure of a barbecued meal is its informality. No one can stand on dignity while prodding a soya sausage with a fork or munching a skewerful of vegetable chunks. For a large barbecue party at which selected cooks do all the actual barbecuing, it may be fun to plan a theme, such as a 'Wild West Rodeo' or 'Hawaiian Sunset Feast' with a suitable menu. But most people enjoy an ordinary barbecue just as much.

Whatever size of party you plan and no matter who you invite, make sure you provide certain simple essentials for success. These are: adequate lighting, plenty of space and easy access to the Cook's Table and barbecue, a bar at some distance from them with plentiful supplies of soft as well as alcoholic drinks, and of course ample supplies of food. Barbecuing makes everyone surprisingly hungry. Make sure you have enough tools for everyone to use who can get round the fire.

Try to provide cushions, garden seats or a couple of groundsheets, so that people waiting to barbecue or equipped with a plateful of food can sit down. Background music, although not essential, can be pleasant if not too loud.

Lighting

Candles or torches may be a romantic idea for an evening

barbecue, but they blow out easily in even a breath of a breeze and may leave guests stumbling across flower-beds in darkness. Fairy lights in the trees look pretty at a distance but only offer a flare-path to mosquitos. Light your barbecue scene with sturdy storm lanterns or site the barbecue near enough to the house for the light inside to illuminate the scene. It is particularly important to have the bar and the barbecue well lit. Pouring drinks in the half-dark can be hazardous, and cooking even more so.

Space

If people choose their own kebabs, burgers, etc. from the Cook's Table, they usually like to spend a moment or two making their choice and selecting seasonings to go with them. The same goes for salads and breads on the serving-table. Allow as much table-space as you can for spreading out foods and place seating (groundsheets, etc.) at some distance from the serving table. Allow ample uncluttered space around the drinks table or bar too. It is a good idea to place one or two small tables holding 'nibbles' where you arrange the seating, to keep people occupied while they wait for drinks or for a turn at the barbecue.

Food

Besides being well lit, the foods on the Cook's Table and serving-table must be clearly labelled, especially if your guests include both meat-eaters and vegetarians. It may be easy to identify a beef steak or a kebab with cubes of pork on it, but it is much less easy to say for sure what a burger or a simmered rice dish contains. Play safe on marinades, bastes and sauces if you have any vegetarian guests. Do not use meat products in any of them; there is no need. All the recipes in this book are suitable for use with meat or vegetables.

Be kind to vegans and save yourself answering dozens of questions by labelling foods free of any animal products with a large V. Paint it on the side of the dish or container with nail polish or shoe paint; both come off easily with the appropriate solvent and provide a more secure form of labelling than a sandwich flag or cardboard label which is likely to disappear in the course of serving.

COOKING ON YOUR BARBECUE

There are five main ways of cooking on your barbecue:

grilling (broiling) on the greased bars of your barbecue grill or in a metal 'net' or double-sided grill (page 6) laid on the bars;

kebab or skewer cooking, also done on the greased bars of the grill, or for safe cooking in a barbecue grill tray (page 7);

frying, either in a frying pan (skillet) or on a flat griddle pan (page 7) which needs only a mere film of oil; and also stir-frying, ideally done in a wok although a deep frying-pan will do;

simmering foods with liquid in a heavy pan with a heat-resistant, non-metal handle; other foods can be reheated or kept warm in a steaming container on top (or just over simmering water);

baking in foil 'parcels' placed on the greased bars of the barbecue grill.

If you have a 'kettle'-style barbecue, you can also bake or 'roast' from scratch foods which need long cooking such as large baking potatoes, sweet potatoes or yams, a whole stuffed vegetable marrow (squash) or a casseroled vegetable stew. But unless you have a second barbecue on which you can grill at the same time, you may lose half the fun of a barbecued meal because the 'kettle' will have to be covered with its lid while the foods cook; in effect, you will be treating your barbecue as an oven. 'Kettle' cooking is ideal for producing a single dish, say a curry, for a large party, but not for creating the camaraderie that sharing the cooking space and tools around an open grill provides.

Preparing your foods

Whatever cooking methods you choose, use only top-quality vegetables and other foods for barbecuing. Do not kid yourself that, because a barbecue meal is informal, less-than-first-class vegetables will do. Remember that they will be cooked over direct heat which may vary (unlike your kitchen cooker heat) in different places on the grill from time to time and that guest cooks may not be used to barbecue cooking. Give them the best possible chance to produce a first-class meal by providing first-class ingredients.

Prepare all your vegetables exactly as you do when preparing them for kitchen cooking. Wash or scrub and dry them. Top and tail, peel or scrape and cut them up if necessary. Some vegetables, e.g. for kebabs, will have to be cut up ahead of time and laid on trays or platters on the Cook's Table at the barbecue, even though it is not ideal nutritionally; marinate such vegetables if you can, to prevent them being exposed to air.

Your food preparation for vegetarians will differ in one respect from those of meat-eating barbecuers. They cook almost all meats from raw on the barbecue. But many vegetables, including some of the tastiest, only become tender and pleasant to eat if they are blanched or, in some cases, partly or fully cooked in liquid or steam before being grilled or fried. Remember to allow time for this when planning your preparations.

Cooking your food

The recipes in this book tell you whether the ingredients need preparing or cooking in the kitchen. It is a good idea to write beside each chosen recipe how much kitchen work it will involve. Unless you have help, do not choose more than two dishes needing last-minute kitchen cooking or you will never get to the barbecue yourself.

At the barbecue, see that the centre of the fire and the grill (broiler) rack are both very hot before you or your guests start cooking. For a start, place the rack 10–15 cm/4–6 inches above the coals. This gives you well-browned grilled or fried foods quickly; you can raise the rack after browning the food surfaces, to complete the tenderising of the foods more slowly if needed. Oil the bars of the rack before you start cooking. Turn the foods with tongs or a broad spatula if you do not use a double-sided hinged grill or a 'net'.

Since vegetarian foods tend to be softer in texture than meats, have plenty of cardboard plates on which to put cooked foods as soon as they are ready. Condiments, any secondary vegetables, salads and relishes should be placed on a serving table nearby so that they can be added to the plates right away. Each diner can then get a plateful of tasty hot food — say a kebab, hot rice and salad — quickly and easily.

Here are some extra notes on the various cooking methods used in barbecuing to make your cooking simple and trouble-free.

1. *Grills* (Broiling) Since most vegetable items have little or no fat content, make sure that burgers and kebabs are particularly well basted during grilling. Use a brush or mop for basting; never pour a baste directly from a jug onto any food because drips will make the fire sputter.

2. *Kebabs* Pieces of vegetable and fruit often slip round on skewers so that the same side always faces the heat. Balance the pieces of food on the skewers carefully and anchor them if possible with small wooden cocktail sticks (toothpicks). Also take care to choose foods for kebabs which will cook in the same time; do not risk some being charred and others half-raw. Remember to choose vivid, varied colours to put on each skewer.

3. *'Fry-ups' and Stir-fries* Put the oil for frying in a jug ahead of time and place it, clearly labelled, on the Cook's Table; a greasy bottle can slip from one's grasp over the fire with disastrous results.

Make a list of all the ingredients needed for a stir-fry and put the items on a tray ahead of time. Tick them off against the recipe before taking the tray to the barbecue. You will not be able to dash back to the kitchen for a special sauce once you have started stir-frying.

4. *Barbecue simmerers* Soups and sauces can easily be reheated or kept warm on the barbecue. However, it is usually more sensible to heat them ahead of time and keep them hot in vacuum flasks, to save space on the barbecue. Rice, pasta etc. can also be reheated or kept hot on the barbecue in a cloth-lined colander over a pan of simmering water if you have room.

Some dishes which only need cooking gently for a fairly short time can even be cooked 'from scratch' on the barbecue. Dishes which need long cooking are safer if almost completed in the kitchen. Just transfer them to the barbecue for the last few minutes.

5. *Foil-wrapped barbecued 'parcels'* One big merit of foil packets is that they can be prepared, seasoned and packed completely ready for cooking ahead of time. Another advantage is that foil packages hold their heat for a long time, so they can be cooked early on the grill (broiler) or the coals and set aside for people waiting to grill or for latecomers.

Vegetable and fruit 'parcels' make a delicious moist addition to grilled or fried foods but take care not to add too much stock or juice to the ingredients, especially to 'watery' vegetables. Unwary diners may be spattered by messy spills.

Use a generous piece of greased foil for each package and fold it securely over the food to prevent any juices seeping out. Try to avoid making thick double folds of foil which may prevent heat reaching the food evenly.

If you serve foil-baked potatoes, mark the containers holding the fillings clearly. Encourage diners to make their choice before they grab their hot potato and juggle with it. As a convenient addition, burger buns split and filled with Herb Baste (page 53) or garlic butter before being wrapped in foil and heated are excellent with barbecued foods.

6. *Other cooks' cooking* If guests or the family will cook for themselves, make sure that your gear includes enough tongs and other tools including heavy-duty gloves for everyone to use. Lay the foods ready for barbecuing on trays with plenty of space between items such as burgers. Make sure, too, that jugs, vacuum flasks, etc. are clearly labelled to show what they contain. Include a few jars of spices, herb-flavoured mustards and pickles for those who like hotter or spicier flavourings than given in the recipes. Finally, just in case of a small accident, have a tube of burn salve handy.

In this book, I have only been able to give you a few of the immensely wide range of vegetarian dishes suitable for barbecue cooking. The cuisines of India and South East Asia and the Far East offer hundreds of such dishes as do the recipes of the Carribean and Latin American peoples. Because of their climate, barbecuing is, for many of them, a natural and commonplace way to cook; and vegetable foods feature largely because they are the most plentiful and cheapest foods available. I hope therefore that, once you have decided that vegetarian barbecuing is both possible and pleasant, you will supplement these recipes with your own 'finds' from the various cuisines of East and West.

Meanwhile, if this is a new adventure for you in party-giving or family meals, good luck and happy eating.

GOOD FOODS FOR BARBECUING

1. You can use every edible plant that grows. But remember that vegetables which need long cooking in the kitchen will need pre-cooking before being barbecued.

2. **Recipes suitable for vegans are marked Ⓥ**. Sometimes a choice of butter or margarine occurs in them; every recipe in this book *can* be made with a margarine free of all animal and dairy products.

3. In recipes using cheese, vegetable-rennet or low-fat hard or soft cheeses can be used.

4. 100% wholemeal (whole wheat) flour is used in most recipes. 81% or 85% extraction flour is suggested for one or two recipes which need to be light in texture.

5. Use a light, pure oil such as corn, peanut or sunflower oil for frying and in most other recipes. Olive oil is suggested for a few dishes.

6. In all recipes, you can substitute other vegetables of a similar type and texture if they are more common, cheaper or freshly in season. Since the dishes will not taste the same, you may need or wish to alter any herbs, spices and seasoning used in them. Make your vegetarian barbecue cookery a creative art.

Notes on Recipe Measures and Servings

Metric, imperial and American measures are given in three separate columns. These measures are not equivalent, so only use one column of measures when following a recipe.

All spoon measures are level; dry goods should be levelled with the rim of the spoon using a knife blade. Use measuring spoons available in most kitchen stores.

All the recipes in the book are designed to serve four people unless otherwise specified.

Recipes for vegans can be used by anyone.

PREPARE AHEAD OF TIME

DRINKS AND NIBBLES

SPICED TOMATO JUICE Ⓥ

Serves 6–8

INGREDIENTS	Metric	Imperial	American
Whole cloves	4	4	4
Celery sticks (stalks), tops with leaves	3	3	3
Tomato juice	750 ml	1¼ pints	3 cups
Water	225 ml	8 fl oz	1 cup
Granulated sugar	1 tbsp	1 tbsp	1 tbsp
Soy sauce	1 tsp	1 tsp	1 tsp
Cayenne pepper	pinch	pinch	dash
Salt	¼ tsp	¼ tsp	¼ tsp
Lemon juice	2 tsp	2 tsp	2 tsp

Tie the cloves and celery tops in a scrap of cloth.

Place all the ingredients in a saucepan and simmer, uncovered, for 20 minutes. Strain into a jug and cool. Cover and chill in the refrigerator.

Store in the refrigerator in a jar with a well-fitting lid. Use within 3 days.

BARBECUERS' CLARET PUNCH Ⓥ

Serves about 12

INGREDIENTS	Metric	Imperial	American
Caster (superfine) sugar	100 g	4 oz	½ cup
Lemon juice	120 ml	4 fl oz	½ cup
Claret or other red wine	1.75 litres	3 pints	7½ cups
Cherry brandy	75 ml	3 fl oz	⅓ cup
Canned red cherries and mandarin orange segments, drained, to decorate			
Soda water	1 litre	1¾ pints	4½ cups

Dissolve the sugar in the lemon juice in a saucepan over gentle heat. Cool.

Mix with the claret and cherry brandy in a well-chilled bowl. Add fruit to decorate and the soda water just before serving.

MULLED CIDER Ⓥ

Serves 6

INGREDIENTS	Metric	Imperial	American
Medium dry cider	1.2 litres	2 pints	5 cups
Soft dark brown sugar	40 g	1½ oz	¼ cup
Salt	pinch	pinch	pinch
Whole cloves	4	4	4
Piece of cinnamon stick	5 cm	2 inch	2 inch
Allspice berries	4	4	4
Orange peel strip	1	1	1

Place the cider, sugar and salt in a large saucepan. Tie the spices in a piece of cloth and add to the pan. Bring slowly to the boil. Cover and simmer gently for 12–15 minutes.

Serve hot in mugs.

GOLDEN TEA PUNCH Ⓥ

Serves 20–24

INGREDIENTS	Metric	Imperial	American
Sweetened lime juice	300 ml	½ pint	1¼ cups
Orange juice	600 ml	1 pint	2½ cups
Hot black tea	600 ml	1 pint	2½ cups
Pineapple juice	900 ml	1½ pints	3¾ cups
Ginger ale	1.2 litres	2 pints	5 cups
Warmed honey to taste			

Mix all the ingredients just before serving. Pour over 2 or 3 large chunks of ice.

Thirst-quenching for barbecuers and ideal for drivers.

ITALIAN MUSHROOMS

INGREDIENTS	Metric	Imperial	American
Button mushrooms	**450 g**	**1 lb**	**1 lb**
Salt	**1 tsp**	**1 tsp**	**1 tsp**
Garlic clove	**1**	**1**	**1**
Fresh bay leaves (or 1 dried leaf)	**2**	**2**	**2**
Medium-sized onion	**1**	**1**	**1**
Water	**350 ml**	**12 fl oz**	**1½ cups**
White wine vinegar	**350 ml**	**12 fl oz**	**1½ cups**
Black peppercorns	**8**	**8**	**8**
Whole cloves	**2**	**2**	**2**
Olive oil as needed			

Sterilise a jar with a screw-top lid which holds 450 ml/¾ pint/ 2 cups liquid.

Cut the stems off the mushrooms and discard. Rinse the caps. Place the caps in a non-metallic saucepan with the salt, garlic, 1 bay leaf (or ½ dried leaf) and the onion.

Bring the water and vinegar to the boil in a second pan and pour the liquid over the mushrooms. Bring back to the boil and simmer for 4 minutes. Drain and cool in a colander.

Take out the garlic, bay leaf and onion, then pack the mushrooms into the sterilised jar. Add the unused bay leaf, peppercorns and cloves. Fill up the jar with olive oil. Close tightly and store for 6 weeks before use.

Serve single mushrooms on cocktail sticks (toothpicks) as 'nibbles' or offer half a jarful as a relish with barbecued foods.

Note: The discarded mushroom stems can be used to flavour a soup or casserole.

DUNKERS AND DIPS

Egg and Parsley Dip

INGREDIENTS	Metric	Imperial	American
Hard-boiled (hard-cooked) eggs, finely chopped	3	3	3
Small spring onion (scallion) bulb, finely chopped	1	1	1
Finely chopped fresh parsley	1 tbsp	1 tbsp	1 tbsp
Dried thyme	pinch	pinch	pinch
Natural (plain) yogurt	3 tbsp	3 tbsp	3 tbsp
Mayonnaise (page 41)	6 tbsp	6 tbsp	6 tbsp
Salt and freshly ground black pepper			

Mix the eggs, spring onion and herbs in a bowl.

Blend the yogurt into the mayonnaise and stir into the egg mixture. Season to taste.

Note: Some cooks add a pinch of grated lemon rind (zest) or nutmeg.

Piccalilli Dip Ⓥ

INGREDIENTS	Metric	Imperial	American
Piccalilli mustard (pickle relish)	175 g	6 oz	¾ cup
Natural (plain) yogurt	225 ml	8 fl oz	1 cup
Salt and freshly ground black pepper			

Chop the piccalilli finely, mix in the yogurt and season to taste.

Guacamole

INGREDIENTS	Metric	Imperial	American
Ripe avocado pears	2	2	2
Small onion, grated	½	½	½
Garlic clove, crushed	¼	¼	¼
Lemon juice	1 tbsp	1 tbsp	1 tbsp
Salt			
Chilli (chili) powder to taste			
Mayonnaise (page 41)	75 ml	5 tbsp	⅓ cup

Peel the avocados and remove the stones (pits). Cut the flesh into small pieces. Mash until almost smooth in a food processor or blender with the onion, garlic, lemon juice, a pinch of salt and a pinch of chilli powder. Gradually add more salt and chilli powder until the dip is as hot as you wish.

Turn the dip into a serving bowl and smooth the surface. Cover at once with the mayonnaise to prevent discoloration. Mix the mayonnaise into the dip when ready to serve.

Note: You can reduce or omit the garlic if you wish. A little finely chopped fresh parsley can be added instead.

Dunkers Ⓥ

INGREDIENTS

Cauliflower florets
Salt
Inside sticks (stalks) of
 celery
Small carrots

Cucumber
Radishes
Button mushrooms
Cooked firm asparagus
 spears in season

Blanch trimmed cauliflower florets in boiling salted water for 2–4 minutes.

Scrape celery sticks and carrots if needed. Cut celery, carrot and cucumber lengthways into narrow 'sticks' about 8 cm/3 inches long.

Top and tail radishes, trim mushroom stems and stick wooden cocktail sticks (toothpicks) in both.

Arrange all the vegetables in lines or clumps on a platter with contrasting colours side by side.

Serve with one of the tasty dips here.

MARINATED TOFU Ⓥ

INGREDIENTS	Metric	Imperial	American
Block of firm tofu (see note)	about 283 g	about 10 oz	about 10 oz
Marinade			
Sunflower or corn oil	4 tbsp	4 tbsp	¼ cup
Soy sauce	150 ml	¼ pint	⅔ cup
Red wine vinegar	2 tbsp	2 tbsp	2 tbsp
Soft brown sugar	2 tbsp	2 tbsp	2 tbsp
Dry mustard powder	¼ tsp	¼ tsp	¼ tsp
Fresh ginger root, grated	1 tbsp	1 tbsp	1 tbsp
Large garlic clove, squeezed	1	1	1

Drain the block of tofu on a tilted plate while you make the marinade.

For the marinade, mix the ingredients in the order given. Add more sugar if you want a sweet-sour mix.

Slice the drained block of tofu in half horizontally if it is more than 3 cm/1 inch thick. (It is usually brick-shaped.) Place the block in a container which just holds it; slices can be side by side or one on top of the other. Pour the marinade over the tofu.

Leave the tofu in the refrigerator for at least 24 hours, turning it over several times to soak both sides thoroughly.

To serve as cocktail 'nibbles' or as an ingredient for stir-fried dishes or salads, cut sliced tofu into small cubes before marinating.

Note: Tofu is high-protein, low-fat soybean curd available in most Health Food Stores.

BLUE CHEESE BITES

Makes about 30 cocktail crackers

INGREDIENTS	Metric	Imperial	American
Blue cheese without rind, crumbled	75 g	3 oz	½ cup
81% extraction flour	75 g	3 oz	¾ cup
Unsalted butter, softened	75 g	3 oz	⅓ cup
Egg, beaten (optional)	2 tbsp	2 tbsp	2 tbsp
Freshly ground black pepper			
Natural (plain) yogurt for brushing			
Celery seeds, to garnish			

With an electric or rotary beater (or in a food processor), blend together the cheese, flour and butter to make a soft, sticky dough. Beat in the egg if using and pepper to taste.

Chill the dough for one hour. Divide it in half. Leaving one half chilled, roll out the other to a thickness of 3 mm/⅛ inch between sheets of greaseproof (wax) paper. Cut into rounds with a 5 cm/2 inch floured cutter. Re-roll and re-cut trimmings.

Place the crackers on ungreased baking sheets. Brush with yogurt and sprinkle with celery seeds.

Bake at 180°C/350°F/Gas Mark 4 for 12–15 minutes or until crisp and browned. Cool on a wire rack, then store in an airtight container.

Repeat the process using the second portion of dough.

BREADS AND ROLLS

OATCAKES Ⓥ

Makes 8 oatcakes

INGREDIENTS	Metric	Imperial	American
Fine oatmeal	175 g	6 oz	1½ cups
81 or 85% extraction (bread) flour	50 g	2 oz	½ cup
Salt	½ tsp	½ tsp	½ tsp
Bicarbonate of soda (baking soda)	¼ tsp	¼ tsp	¼ tsp
Margarine	25 g	1 oz	2 tbsp
Hot water	75–120 ml	3–4 fl oz	⅓ to ½ cup

Fine oatmeal for dusting

Mix together the oatmeal, flour, salt and soda in a bowl. Melt the margarine and add to the dry ingredients with enough hot water to make a stiff dough.

Turn onto a board dusted with oatmeal and knead until smooth. Divide the dough into 2 equal portions. Roll them out into large rounds as thinly as possible, dusting with oatmeal to prevent them sticking; pinch the edges to keep them even. Cut each round into 4 quarters. Place on an ungreased baking sheet dusted with oatmeal.

Bake at 180°C/350°F/Gas Mark 4 for about 20 minutes until the edges begin to brown. Cool on the sheets and store in an airtight container.

To serve, dust with oatmeal, then toast lightly on the barbecue.

BURGER BUNS OR LONG ROLLS

Makes 12 buns or rolls

INGREDIENTS	Metric	Imperial	American
Milk	120 ml	4 fl oz	½ cup
Water	120 ml	4 fl oz	½ cup
Clear honey	1½ tsp	1½ tsp	1½ tsp
Dried yeast (see method)	1½ tsp	1½ tsp	1½ tsp
Strong white flour (bread flour) or 81% extraction flour	350 g	12 oz	3 cups
Salt	1 tsp	1 tsp	1 tsp

Mix the milk and water in a saucepan. Warm to hand-hot. Stir in the honey. If using plain yeast, sprinkle the yeast on top and leave until frothy.

Sift the flour and salt into a bowl, then add the frothy yeasted liquid. If using yeast with added Vitamin C, add to the sifted flour and salt, then mix in the warmed milk, water and honey.

Mix well with a wooden spoon, then by hand until the mixture sticks together. It may be quite sticky. Turn out onto a floured surface and knead until smooth. Return the dough to the bowl and cover loosely with oiled polythene (plastic). Leave in a warm place until doubled in bulk.

Punch the dough down, knead again for a few moments until smooth, then divide into 12 equal portions. Roll each into a smooth ball.

Place well apart on a greased baking sheet. Flatten to a thickness of about 2 cm/¾ inch with your palm. Leave in a warm place until puffy.

Bake at 200°C/400°F/Gas Mark 6 for 15–20 minutes. Cool on a wire rack.

For *long rolls*, shape the dough into cylinders instead of balls but do not flatten them. Prove and bake them like round buns. Cool in a cloth on a wire rack. Split and fill with Vegetarian 'Sausages' (page 55) or with a savoury spread or salad.

PITTA BREADS

Makes 4

INGREDIENTS	Metric	Imperial	American
Clear honey	½ tsp	½ tsp	½ tsp
Warm water	300 ml	½ pint	1¼ cups
Fresh (compressed) yeast	25 g	1 oz	1 cake
Strong white flour (bread flour) or 81% extraction flour	450 g	1 lb	4 cups
Salt	2 tsp	2 tsp	2 tsp
Olive oil	2 tbsp	2 tbsp	2 tbsp
Extra oil as needed			

Dissolve the honey in half the water. Blend in the yeast. Leave until a soft curd forms on the water.

Mix the flour and salt in a bowl. Make a hollow in the centre and pour in the yeast liquid. Add the remaining water and oil. Mix all the ingredients with a wooden spoon to make a soft dough.

Knead for a full 8 minutes by hand or use a dough hook or food processor and knead for 6 minutes. Shape the dough into an oval. Rub it with oil and cover with a cloth. Leave in a warm place for about 1 hour or until doubled in bulk.

Punch the dough down and knead out any creases. Divide it into 4 equal-sized pieces. Roll into balls and leave to rise again, uncovered, for 30 minutes.

Roll out the balls into ovals 3 mm/⅛ inch thick. Lay on greased and floured baking sheets. Leave for another 30 minutes.

Bake at 240°C/475°F/Gas Mark 9 for 10–12 minutes. Wrap in a cloth immediately to soften the breads, and cool on a wire rack.

Reheat gently in foil if you wish on the edge of the barbecue.

COURGETTE AND MUSTARD BREAD

Makes 12–16 slices

INGREDIENTS	Metric	Imperial	American
Plain (all-purpose) flour	175 g	6 oz	1½ cups
Baking powder	2 tsp	2 tsp	2 tsp
Salt	1 tsp	1 tsp	1 tsp
Caster (superfine) sugar	2 tsp	2 tsp	2 tsp
Courgettes (zucchini), grated	175 g	6 oz	1½ cups
Walnut pieces, chopped	75 g	3 oz	¾ cup
Eggs	2	2	2
Sunflower or other light oil	4 tbsp	4 tbsp	4 tbsp
French mustard	3 tbsp	3 tbsp	3 tbsp

Sift the dry ingredients into a bowl. Add the courgettes and nuts. Beat together the eggs, oil and mustard and stir into the mixture until evenly distributed. Turn the mixture into a greased 20 × 10 cm/8 × 4 inch bread tin (loaf pan).

Bake at 180°C/350°F/Gas Mark 4 for 1 hour, until well risen and firm. Cool slightly, then remove from the tin (pan) and finish cooling on a wire rack.

Serve cold, sliced and spread with butter.

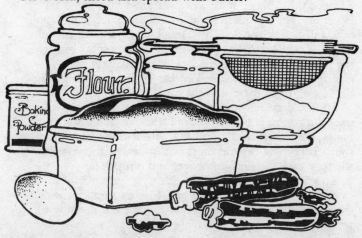

SALADS AND DRESSINGS

PINEAPPLE SLAW

INGREDIENTS	Metric	Imperial	American
Firm white cabbage	600 g	1¼ lb	1¼ lb
Fresh pineapple, about 900 g/2 lb weight	1	1	1
Sharp dessert apple	1	1	1
Walnut halves	75 g	3 oz	¾ cup
Dressing			
Mayonnaise (page 41)	4 tbsp	4 tbsp	¼ cup
Natural (plain) yogurt	120 ml	4 fl oz	½ cup
Salt and white pepper			
Clear honey	2 tsp	2 tsp	2 tsp
Lemon or orange juice to taste			

Remove the cabbage stalk and any coarse ribs. Shred the leaves finely. Peel, quarter and core the pineapple and apple over a dish. Cut the flesh into small cubes, adding any juice collected while cutting the pineapple. Toss both fruits with the juice to coat the apple cubes, then mix with the cabbage. Reserve 6 or 8 walnut halves for garnishing. Chop the rest and mix them into the salad.

For the dressing, stir together the mayonnaise and yogurt until the yogurt is liquid. Add a little seasoning. Stir in the honey, then sharpen the dressing with lemon or orange juice; the quantity will depend on the sharpness of the yogurt. Toss the slaw with the dressing, cover and refrigerate.

To serve, toss again and garnish with walnut halves.

You can make this slaw up to 24 hours ahead, provided the apple cubes are well coated with juice and dressing to prevent discoloration.

ITALIAN MIXED SALAD

INGREDIENTS	Metric	Imperial	American
Garlic clove (optional)	½	½	½
Head of cos (romaine) lettuce cut lengthways	¼	¼	¼
Small head of radicchio or young spinach	½	½	½
Small onion, grated	1	1	1
Chopped fresh parsley	1 tbsp	1 tbsp	1 tbsp
Salt and freshly ground black pepper			
Unpeeled cucumber, sliced	¼	¼	¼
Medium-sized tomatoes cut into wedges	2	2	2
Red radishes, sliced	6–8	6–8	6–8
Green pepper, de-seeded and cut into small thin strips	¼	¼	¼
Capers, drained	2 tbsp	2 tbsp	2 tbsp
French Dressing (page 39)			

Rub the inside of a shallow salad bowl with the cut side of a garlic clove if you wish (see note).

Shred the lettuce and radicchio or spinach. Mix them in the bowl with the onion and parsley, and season to taste.

Arrange the cucumber, tomato, radishes and pepper in 4 separate sections or groups on top. Season again and sprinkle with the capers. Cover with cling film (plastic wrap) and chill for up to 3 hours.

Just before serving, sprinkle with dressing.

Note: If you do not use garlic, rub the inside of the bowl with walnut oil and use it to make the dressing as well.

CARROT AND ORANGE SALAD Ⓥ

INGREDIENTS	Metric	Imperial	American
Young carrots	450 g	1 lb	1 lb
Chopped fresh parsley	1 tbsp	1 tbsp	1 tbsp
Freshly ground black pepper			
Orange juice (freshly squeezed or from carton)	3 tbsp	3 tbsp	3 tbsp
Lemon juice	2 tsp	2 tsp	2 tsp

Grate or shred the carrots but not too finely. Mix with the parsley in a salad bowl. Grind pepper over the top to taste. Toss these ingredients with the juices shortly before serving.

CALCUTTA CLUB SALAD

INGREDIENTS	Metric	Imperial	American
Long grain rice	100 g	4 oz	generous ½ cup
Salt			
Frozen cut green beans, blanched and drained	100 g	4 oz	1 cup
Button mushrooms, sliced	50 g	2 oz	⅔ cup
Piece of cucumber, diced	5 cm	2 inches	2 inches
Curry paste	1–2 tsp	1–2 tsp	1–2 tsp
Mayonnaise (page 41)	3 tbsp	3 tbsp	3 tbsp

Cook the rice in boiling salted water until tender. Drain and rinse under cold water. Cool.

Mix together the rice, beans, mushrooms and cucumber in a bowl. Blend the curry paste into the mayonnaise and toss with the salad. Chill before serving.

BEAN SPROUT AND PASTA SALAD Ⓥ

INGREDIENTS	Metric	Imperial	American
Wholemeal (whole wheat) pasta shapes	175 g	6 oz	1½ cups
Salt			
Canned pineapple slices in natural juice	227 g	8 oz	8¼ oz
Carrots, shredded	2	2	2
Cucumber, sliced	½	½	½
Bean sprouts (see note)	175 g	6 oz	3 cups
Dressing			
Corn oil	120 ml	4 fl oz	½ cup
Orange juice	2 tbsp	2 tbsp	2 tbsp
Pineapple juice, reserved from can	2 tbsp	2 tbsp	2 tbsp
Soy sauce	1 tbsp	1 tbsp	1 tbsp
Ground ginger	pinch	pinch	pinch

Boil the pasta shapes in plenty of salted water until just tender.

Meanwhile drain the pineapple, reserving the juice. Cut the slices into small pieces and set aside.

Combine all the ingredients for the dressing. Drain the pasta when ready and mix with the dressing while still warm. Cool completely.

Add the carrots, cucumber and pineapple and toss. Lastly fork in the bean sprouts lightly.

Note: Several kinds of sprouts, with or without the beans or seeds, are now available in vacuum packs. Use any kind except alfalfa sprouts, which are too thin and fine for this salad.

RAINBOW SALAD Ⓥ

INGREDIENTS	Metric	Imperial	American
Dressing			
Olive oil	8 tbsp	8 tbsp	8 tbsp
Lemon juice	4 tbsp	4 tbsp	4 tbsp
Caster (superfine) sugar	½ tsp	½ tsp	½ tsp
Salt	1 tsp	1 tsp	1 tsp
Freshly ground pepper (any kind)			
Salad			
Carrots, grated	2	2	2
Button mushrooms, sliced	100 g	4 oz	1 cup
Cucumber, de-seeded and cut into 'matchsticks'	½	½	½
Tomatoes, quartered	5	5	5
Celery sticks (stalks), sliced	4	4	4
Garnish			
Spring onions (scallions), chopped	2	2	2
Chopped chives	1 tbsp	1 tbsp	1 tbsp
Chopped fresh parsley	1 tbsp	1 tbsp	1 tbsp
Onion rings			

Make the dressing first, by mixing together all the ingredients.

Toss the carrot in a bowl with 2 tablespoons of the dressing. Arrange in a strip on a flat platter.

Lay the mushrooms, cucumber, tomatoes and celery in strips alongside it. Sprinkle each with one of the garnishes.

Serve the rest of the dressing separately in a jug.

RAW MUSHROOM SALAD Ⓥ

INGREDIENTS	Metric	Imperial	American
Large equal-sized button mushrooms	225 g	8 oz	½ lb
Soy Dressing (page 41) made with 120 ml/ 4 fl oz/½ cup water			

Cut off the mushroom stems level with the cap bases and discard. (The discarded stems can be used for flavouring a soup or casserole.) Slice the caps thinly. Arrange the slices in a single layer of overlapping concentric rings in a flat shallow dish.

Pour the diluted dressing over them gently, making sure they are all coated. If necessary tilt the dish and baste with dressing from the side.

Allow to marinate for at least 1 hour before serving, longer if possible.

MIXED PULSE SALAD

INGREDIENTS	Metric	Imperial	American
Can of chickpeas (garbanzos)	400 g	14 oz	16 oz
Can of red kidney beans	425 g	15 oz	16 oz
Can of sweetcorn kernels	198 g	7 oz	8 oz
Green Onion Dressing (page 40)	3–4 tbsp	3–4 tbsp	3–4 tbsp

Drain all the cans well. Mix together the chickpeas, beans and sweetcorn in a bowl.

To serve, toss with the dressing.

GREEK POTATO SALAD

INGREDIENTS	Metric	Imperial	American
New potatoes, boiled and diced	350 g	12 oz	2 cups
Medium-sized tomatoes, skinned, de-seeded and chopped	225 g	8 oz	1 cup
Onion, finely chopped	1	1	1
Black olives, stoned (pitted)	50 g	2 oz	¼ cup
Mayonnaise (page 41)	3 tbsp	3 tbsp	3 tbsp
Milk or natural (plain) yogurt	2 tbsp	2 tbsp	2 tbsp
Freshly ground black pepper			

Toss together the potatoes, tomatoes, onion and olives.

Mix the mayonnaise with the milk or yogurt and add pepper to taste. Toss with the vegetables, coating them evenly.

Chill before serving.

CUCUMBER AND WALNUT SALAD Ⓥ

INGREDIENTS	Metric	Imperial	American
Cucumbers	450 g	1 lb	1 lb
Red radishes	8	8	8
Large green pepper	1	1	1
Spring onion (scallion) (green and white parts)	1	1	1
Walnut pieces	50 g	2 oz	½ cup
Dried thyme	¼ tsp	¼ tsp	¼ tsp
Chopped fresh parsley	1 tsp	1 tsp	1 tsp
Quarter recipe quantity Soy Dressing (page 41), made with water			

Put the ingredients straight into your salad bowl as you prepare them.

Halve the cucumbers lengthways, then slice them across into thin half-moons. Top and tail the radishes and slice them thinly.

Halve and core the pepper, removing most of the seeds; leave a few for their 'bite'. Chop the pepper, spring onion and walnut pieces together coarsely, and add them to the bowl with the herbs. Cover and chill if the salad must wait.

To serve, toss the salad with enough dressing to moisten it lightly and flavour it.

FRENCH DRESSING

INGREDIENTS	Metric	Imperial	American
Corn, groundnut or other light oil (see note)	2–3 tbsp	2–3 tbsp	2–3 tbsp
Dry mustard powder	pinch	pinch	pinch
Salt and freshly ground black pepper			
Wine vinegar (see note)	1 tbsp	1 tbsp	1 tbsp

Mix together the oil and seasonings to taste in a bowl. Whisk (beat) in the vinegar drop by drop to form an emulsion. Whisk again just before use.

Alternatively you can shake the oil and seasonings in a small jar with a secure stopper; add the vinegar and shake again briskly. Repeat just before use.

Note: Heavy or strongly flavoured oils such as olive oil should not be used for delicate green leaf salads; they make them soggy. These oils, like malt vinegar, should be kept for dressing strongly flavoured leaf salads such as chicory (endive). A dressing for very delicate leaves or for salads containing fruits is best made partly or wholly with lemon juice instead of all vinegar.

For many mixed salads, garlic oil or a herb vinegar are delicious in a dressing.

YOGURT DRESSING

Makes 150 ml/¼ pt/⅔ cup

INGREDIENTS	Metric	Imperial	American
Natural (plain) yogurt	120 ml	4 fl oz	½ cup
Soured (sour) cream	2 tbsp	2 tbsp	2 tbsp
Mixed English or American mustard	¼ tsp	¼ tsp	¼ tsp
Lemon juice	1 tbsp	1 tbsp	1 tbsp
Salt and black pepper			

Stir the yogurt until smooth and liquid. Blend in all the remaining ingredients. Taste and adjust the seasoning if you wish. Cover and chill until needed.

GREEN ONION DRESSING

INGREDIENTS	Metric	Imperial	American
Mayonnaise (page 41)	120 ml	4 fl oz	½ cup
Natural (plain) yogurt	4 tbsp	4 tbsp	¼ cup
Spring onion (scallion) (green and white parts) cut in 3 cm/1 inch lengths	1	1	1
White wine vinegar	½ tbsp	½ tbsp	½ tbsp
Lemon juice	1 tsp	1 tsp	1 tsp
Large parsley sprigs, leaves only	2	2	2
Sugar (optional)	pinch	pinch	pinch
Salt	small pinch	small pinch	small pinch
Cayenne pepper	small pinch	small pinch	small pinch
Garlic clove	½	½	½

Place all the ingredients except the garlic into a blender in the order given. Squeeze the garlic over, through a garlic press. Cover and blend until the onions and parsley leaves are finely chopped.

Chill, covered, for at least 1 hour before use.

MAYONNAISE

INGREDIENTS	Metric	Imperial	American
Egg	1	1	1
Salt	½ tsp	½ tsp	½ tsp
Dried mustard	¼ tsp	¼ tsp	¼ tsp
White wine vinegar	1 tbsp	1 tbsp	1 tbsp
Corn, sunflower or soya oil: about	225 ml	8 fl oz	1 cup

Place the egg and seasonings in a blender and process at top speed until foamy. Blend in the vinegar. With the motor running, add the oil drop by drop until the mayonnaise thickens. Then add it in a thin ribbon, until the mayonnaise is as thick as you want it. It thickens quickly. Blend in 1 tablespoon boiling water at the end to prevent curdling.

SOY DRESSING ⓥ

INGREDIENTS	Metric	Imperial	American
Soy sauce	4 tbsp	4 tbsp	4 tbsp
Corn oil	1 tbsp	1 tbsp	1 tbsp
Lemon juice	1 tbsp	1 tbsp	1 tbsp
Ground ginger	½ tsp	½ tsp	½ tsp
Clear honey, warmed	4 tsp	4 tsp	4 tsp
Cold water (optional)			

Stir together the soy sauce, oil, lemon juice, ginger and honey in a jug. Use for seasoning kebabs and stir-fries.

If you add water (60–120 ml/2–4 fl oz/¼–½ cup) you can use the diluted mixture for dressing Raw Mushroom Salad (page 37) or Cucumber and Walnut Salad (page 38).

DESSERT FINGER-FOODS

A bowl of mixed fresh fruits is all that is really needed as a cold barbecue dessert. However, many people like a slice of cake or flan or a few cookies to eat with their barbecued hot fruits (page 92).

FRIED APPLE CAKE

Serves 8–10

INGREDIENTS	Metric	Imperial	American
Base			
Unsalted butter	100 g	4 oz	½ cup
Digestive biscuit (graham cracker) crumbs	175 g	6 oz	2¼ cups
Large apples, peeled and sliced	2	2	2
Sultanas (golden raisins)	100 g	4 oz	⅔ cup
Filling			
Gouda cheese, finely grated	250 g	9 oz	2 cups
81% extraction flour	3 tbsp	3 tbsp	3 tbsp
Single (light) cream	4½ tbsp	4½ tbsp	4½ tbsp
Ground mixed spice	½ tsp	½ tsp	½ tsp
Grated rind (zest) and juice of lemon	1	1	1
Eggs, separated	3	3	3
Caster (superfine) sugar	100 g	4 oz	½ cup

Decoration

Red-skinned apples,			
cored and sliced	2	2	2
Apricot jam, sieved	2 tbsp	2 tbsp	2 tbsp

For the base, melt half the butter in a saucepan and stir in the biscuit crumbs. Press the mixture into the base of a loose-bottomed 20 cm/8 inch cake tin (springform cake pan).

Fry the apple slices in the remaining butter until just soft and golden. Drain off any free fat. Cool the apples slightly, then spread over the biscuit crumb base. Scatter the sultanas on top.

For the filling, mix together the cheese, flour, cream, mixed spice, lemon rind and juice. Mix together the egg yolks and sugar and stir into the cheese mixture, blending evenly. Whisk (beat) the egg whites until stiff but not dry and fold in. Turn the cheese mixture gently onto the apples in the tin.

Bake at 180°C/350°F/Gas Mark 4 for 45–50 minutes. Cool in the tin on a wire rack.

When cold, arrange the red-skinned apple slices in rings around the top of the cake. Warm the apricot jam until liquid and brush over the apple rings.

Half-way between a cake and a cheesecake, this cake is firm enough to be eaten without a spoon, yet can equally well be served as a dessert with cream. It makes a super alternative to a classic apple pie and keeps well.

RUM CUSTARD FLAN

Serves 6–8

INGREDIENTS	Metric	Imperial	American
Shortcrust pastry (basic pie dough), made with 175 g/6 oz/1½ cups flour			
Filling			
Milk	250 ml	8 fl oz	1 cup
Eggs, separated	3	3	3
Caster (superfine) sugar	100 g	4 oz	½ cup
Agar agar	1 tsp	1 tsp	1 tsp
Boiling water	4 tbsp	4 tbsp	¼ cup
Vanilla extract or flavouring	1 tbsp	1 tbsp	1 tbsp
Rum	2–3 tbsp	2–3 tbsp	2–3 tbsp
Salt	¼ tsp	¼ tsp	¼ tsp
Grated chocolate (optional)	25 g	1 oz	¼ cup

Make the pastry and use it to line a 23 cm/9 inch flan case or ring. Bake blind at 200°C/400°F/Gas Mark 6 until fully baked.

For the filling, heat the milk in the top of a double boiler over simmering water.

Beat the egg yolks and sugar in a bowl until well blended. Stir in the hot milk. Return the mixture to the double boiler and stir over the hot water until it is the consistency of thick cream. Dissolve the agar agar in the boiling water.

Remove the custard from the heat and stir in the agar agar, then the vanilla and rum. Cool until just beginning to set at the edges of the pan.

Whisk (beat) the egg whites with the salt until they hold soft peaks. Fold into the cooled custard, then spoon the mixture into the cooled pastry case. Chill until well set. Sprinkle with chocolate, if desired.

Note: The pie can be topped with sweetened whipped cream instead of chocolate if you prefer.

GINGERBREAD

INGREDIENTS	Metric	Imperial	American
81 or 85% extraction flour	450 g	1 lb	4 cups
Ground ginger	3 tsp	3 tsp	3 tsp
Baking powder	3 tsp	3 tsp	3 tsp
Bicarbonate of soda (baking soda)	1 tsp	1 tsp	1 tsp
Salt	1 tsp	1 tsp	1 tsp
Demerara (brown) sugar	225 g	8 oz	1⅓ cups
Unsalted butter	175 g	6 oz	¾ cup
Black treacle (molasses)	175 g	6 oz	½ cup
Golden syrup (corn syrup)	175 g	6 oz	½ cup
Egg, beaten	1	1	1
Milk	300 ml	½ pint	1¼ cups

Grease and line a deep 23 cm/9 inch square cake tin (baking pan).

Sift together all the dry ingredients except the sugar into a large bowl.

Place the sugar, butter, treacle and syrup in a saucepan and warm until the butter has just melted. Mix the egg into the milk.

Stir the melted mixture into the middle of the dry ingredients, then mix in the milk. Beat thoroughly with a wooden spoon. Pour the batter into the prepared tin.

Bake at 180°C/350°F/Gas Mark 4 for 1½ hours or until the gingerbread is springy in the centre. Leave to cool in the tin, then turn out onto a wire rack.

When cold, wrap in foil without removing the lining paper. Store for 4–6 days then cut into squares.

Gingerbread is one of the best finger-food desserts to serve at a barbecue. Its spicy flavour complements grilled food perfectly. It is excellent with fruit or cheese or, if you prefer, it can be served with dollops of whipped cream. As a bonus, you can make it almost a week ahead.

CARROT AND ALMOND CAKE

Makes one 18 cm/7 inch round cake

INGREDIENTS	Metric	Imperial	American
Eggs, separated	5	5	5
Light soft brown sugar	200 g	7 oz	7 oz
Lemon juice	1 tbsp	1 tbsp	1 tbsp
Young carrots, grated (about 275 g/10 oz/2½ cups unprepared)	225 g	8 oz	2 cups
Ground almonds	225 g	8 oz	2 cups
81% extraction flour, sifted	4 tbsp	4 tbsp	4 tbsp
Ground cinnamon or mixed spice	1 tsp	1 tsp	1 tsp
Topping			
Melted butter or margarine	2 tbsp	2 tbsp	2 tbsp
Soft brown sugar	65 g	2½ oz	⅓ cup
Single (light) cream	1½ tbsp	1½ tbsp	1½ tbsp
Mixed chopped nuts	75 g	3 oz	¾ cup

Grease and line a deep 18 cm/7 in cake tin (round cake pan).

Beat the egg yolks until frothy. Add the sugar and beat until smooth and creamy. Beat in the lemon juice.

Add and beat in one third of the carrots, then one third of the almonds. Repeat this process twice. Stir in the flour and spice. Whisk the egg whites and fold them in. Turn the mixture into the prepared tin.

Bake at 180°C/350°F/Gas Mark 4 for 1 hour. Cover the cake loosely with greaseproof (waxed) paper and reduce the heat to 160°C/325°F/Gas Mark 3 for 15–20 minutes or until the cake shrinks slightly from the sides of the tin. A skewer inserted into the middle of the cake will still be moist.

Cool the cake in the tin until just warm. Turn out on to a wire rack to finish cooling.

Combine the topping ingredients and cover the cake. Heat under the grill (broiler) until golden-brown.

GIANT SPICY PLATE COOKIES Ⓥ

Makes 10 giant or 20 half-sized cookies

INGREDIENTS	Metric	Imperial	American
81 or 85% extraction flour	275 g	10 oz	2½ cups
Salt	¼ tsp	¼ tsp	¼ tsp
Ground ginger	1 tsp	1 tsp	1 tsp
Ground cloves	pinch	pinch	pinch
Ground allspice	pinch	pinch	pinch
Grated nutmeg	pinch	pinch	pinch
Hot water	2 tbsp	2 tbsp	2 tbsp
Rum	3 tbsp	3 tbsp	3 tbsp
Bicarbonate of soda (baking soda)	½ tsp	½ tsp	½ tsp
Treacle (molasses)	50 ml	2 fl oz	3 tbsp
Vegetable oil	4 tbsp	4 tbsp	¼ cup
Warmed honey or maple syrup	120 ml	4 fl oz	½ cup
Chopped mixed nuts	1½ tbsp	1½ tbsp	1½ tbsp

Sift together the flour, salt and spices into a bowl. Mix the remaining ingredients except the nuts in a jug. Pour onto the dry ingredients and stir to make a smooth dough. Chill for 30–40 minutes.

Grease 2 or 3 large baking sheets.

For giant cookies place mounds of dough 11 cm/4½ inches apart on the sheets and well away from the sides. Press each mound with the flat base of a glass dipped in flour, to flatten it into a 10 cm/4 inch circle about 5 mm/¼ in thick. Sprinkle with nuts.

Bake at 190°C/375°F/Gas Mark 5 for 10 minutes. Loosen, then cool on the sheets.

MARINADES, BASTES AND SAUCES

SOY MARINADE FOR BEAN CURD (TOFU) AND KEBAB FOODS Ⓥ

Makes about 250 ml/8 fl oz/1 cup marinade

INGREDIENTS	Metric	Imperial	American
Soy sauce	5 tbsp	5 tbsp	5 tbsp
Sherry	6 tbsp	6 tbsp	6 tbsp
Sunflower or corn oil	2 tbsp	2 tbsp	2 tbsp
Dried minced garlic	½ tsp	½ tsp	½ tsp
Soft brown sugar	2 tbsp	2 tbsp	2 tbsp
Ground ginger	2 tsp	2 tsp	2 tsp
Dry mustard powder	½ tsp	½ tsp	½ tsp

Mix together all the ingredients in a bowl or jug, whisking (beating) with a fork to blend in the sugar, ginger and mustard.

Use for marinating firm tofu, commercial soya 'sausages' and similar foods or for brushing over kebabs before grilling (broiling). Also useful as a dressing for cooked pulses.

For a stronger-flavoured marinade made with fresh ginger and garlic, see page 26.

WINE MARINADE FOR VEGETABLES Ⓥ

Marinade for 450 g/1 lb vegetables

INGREDIENTS	Metric	Imperial	American
Medium-sized onion, coarsely chopped	1	1	1
Parsley stalks	6	6	6
Thyme or tarragon sprig	1	1	1
Strip of lemon rind (zest) or fresh bay leaf	1	1	1
Dry white wine	450 ml	¾ pint	2 cups
White wine vinegar or lemon juice or a mixture	2 tbsp	2 tbsp	2 tbsp
Warmed clear honey	2 tsp	2 tsp	2 tsp
Sunflower or corn oil	2 tbsp	2 tbsp	2 tbsp
Salt and white pepper to taste			
Cayenne pepper	pinch	pinch	pinch

Tie the onion, parsley stalks, herb sprig and lemon rind or bay leaf loosely in a piece of thin cloth. Mix together all the liquids and seasoning to taste in a large bowl. Add the cloth parcel and soak it in the liquids for approximately 2 hours.

Add the chosen vegetables and turn them in the marinade to coat well. Marinate for 30–60 minutes. Large pieces of raw vegetables and coarse vegetables will need to be marinated the longest. Drain the vegetables well before use.

Note: For delicate vegetables, use only lemon juice instead of wine vinegar.

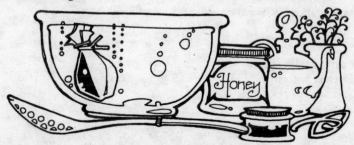

GARLIC MARINADE AND BASTE Ⓥ

Makes about 400 ml/14 fl oz/1¾ cups

INGREDIENTS	Metric	Imperial	American
Dry white wine	300 ml	½ pint	1¼ cups
Olive oil	120 ml	4 fl oz	½ cup
Fresh bay leaves (or 1 dried leaf)	2	2	2
White sugar	½ tsp	½ tsp	½ tsp
Garlic clove, crushed	1	1	1
Salt and freshly ground black pepper			

Mix together the wine and oil in a bowl or jug. Add the bay leaves. Stir in the sugar and garlic. Season to taste.

Use for soaking strongly flavoured vegetables before grilling (broiling) or frying, and for brushing over them while on the grill.

Stir the mixture several times and turn the vegetables over in it from time to time if using it as a marinade.

GARLIC BUTTER OR SAUCE FOR DRESSING VEGETABLES

Makes about 175 g/6 oz/¾ cup butter

INGREDIENTS	Metric	Imperial	American
Large garlic cloves	2	2	2
Butter, softened	175 g	6 oz	¾ cup
Salt and pepper			

Pound or mince the peeled garlic cloves or squeeze them through a garlic press over the butter. Work them into the butter thoroughly. Season to taste. Put in a small pot, cover tightly and chill. Use within 48 hours.

The butter can be rolled into small balls or pats, softened for spreading or melted.

To vary, work into the butter a pinch of dried mustard, a few drops of lemon juice or a pinch of cayenne pepper.

FRESH TOMATO SAUCE Ⓥ

Makes about 900 ml/1½ pint/3¾ cups sauce

INGREDIENTS	Metric	Imperial	American
Corn or other light oil	3 tbsp	3 tbsp	3 tbsp
Medium-sized onion, finely chopped	1	1	1
Celery stick (stalk), finely chopped	1	1	1
Medium-sized carrot, finely chopped	1	1	1
Garlic clove, crushed (optional)	1	1	1
Ripe tomatoes, chopped	1.5 kg	3 lb	3 lb
Water	3 tbsp	3 tbsp	3 tbsp
White sugar	pinch	pinch	pinch
Fresh chopped basil or parsley	1 tsp	1 tsp	1 tsp
Bay leaf	1	1	1
Salt and ground black pepper			

Heat the oil in a saucepan. Add the vegetables and stir over low heat for 5–6 minutes. Add the tomatoes to the pan with the water, sugar, herbs and a little seasoning. Cover the pan and simmer for 15–20 minutes until the tomatoes are reduced to pulp. Remove the bay leaf and rub the vegetables and liquid through a sieve. Adjust the seasoning to taste.

BARBECUE SAUCE FOR BURGERS AND OTHER BARBECUED FOODS (V)

Makes about 300 ml/½ pint/1¼ cups sauce

INGREDIENTS	Metric	Imperial	American
Soft brown sugar	2 tbsp	2 tbsp	2 tbsp
Dijon mustard	5 tsp	5 tsp	5 tsp
Tomato purée	1½ tbsp	1½ tbsp	1½ tbsp
Tomato juice	3 tbsp	3 tbsp	3 tbsp
Lemon juice	1 tbsp	1 tbsp	1 tbsp
Soy sauce	2 tbsp	2 tbsp	2 tbsp
Corn or other light oil	3 tbsp	3 tbsp	3 tbsp
Medium-sized onion, finely chopped	1	1	1
Sharp dessert apple, peeled, cored and finely chopped	1	1	1
Green pepper, de-seeded and finely chopped	½	½	½
Salt and freshly ground black pepper			

In a heavy saucepan, mix together the sugar, mustard and tomato purée. Gradually blend in the tomato juice, lemon juice, soy sauce and oil. Stir the onion, apple and green pepper into the sauce mixture. Season lightly.

Simmer the sauce, uncovered, for 15–20 minutes, stirring occasionally. The onion and fruit should absorb all the oil. Serve hot or cold.

For a smooth sauce, cool, then sieve or process in a blender or food processor. Reheat if you wish, on the barbecue or in the kitchen and keep hot in a food flask.

HERB BASTE FOR VEGETABLES Ⓥ

Makes about 275 g/10 oz/1¼ cups baste

INGREDIENTS	Metric	Imperial	American
Finely chopped fresh parsley	3 tbsp	3 tbsp	3 tbsp
Spring onion (scallion) or shallot, finely chopped (minced)	3 tbsp	3 tbsp	3 tbsp
Dried mixed herbs	1 tsp	1 tsp	1 tsp
Dry mustard powder	½ tsp	½ tsp	½ tsp
Ground black pepper	pinch	pinch	pinch
Chilli (chili) sauce	2–4 drops	2–4 drops	2–4 drops
Butter or margarine, softened	225 g	8 oz	1 cup

Mix all the flavourings into the softened butter or margarine thoroughly. Taste and add extra chilli sauce if desired.

Use to brush over vegetables while grilling (broiling) them.

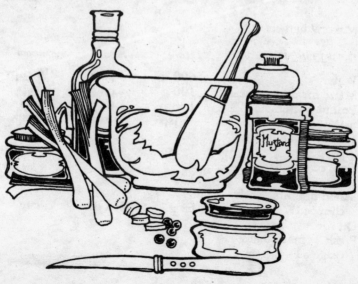

ON YOUR BARBECUE

BURGERS, CUTLETS AND OTHER GRILLED FOODS

NUTTY BURGERS Ⓥ

Makes 9 burgers

INGREDIENTS	Metric	Imperial	American
Water	600 ml	1 pint	2½ cups
Maize meal (cornmeal)	100 g	4 oz	⅔ cup
Peanut butter	1 tbsp	1 tbsp	1 tbsp
Salt	½ tsp	½ tsp	½ tbsp
Freshly ground black pepper	⅛ tsp	⅛ tsp	⅛ tsp
Cooked bulghar (page 80)	175 g	6 oz	6 oz
Salted peanuts, finely chopped	65 g	2½ oz	½ cup
Oil for brushing			
Fresh Tomato Sauce (page 51)			

Bring the water to a boil in a large pan over medium heat. Stir in the maize meal, peanut butter and seasonings. Cover and reduce the heat to very low. Cook for 30 minutes, stirring frequently to prevent the mixture from sticking to the pan. It should be stiff enough to leave the pan clean when a spoon is drawn across it. Cool in the pan, it will stiffen even more.

When just warm, mix in thoroughly the cold bulghar and nuts. Re-season if you wish. Shape the mixture into 9 equal-sized patties. Chill for at least 30 minutes.

At the barbecue, brush the patties with oil. Cook them in a double-sided grill (page 6) until both sides are lightly browned. Alternatively, fry them on a barbecue griddle pan (page 7).

Serve with Fresh Tomato Sauce.

VEGETARIAN 'SAUSAGES'

Any firm burger or patty mixture can be shaped into small rolls or 'sausage' shapes and grilled (broiled) or fried on the barbecue.

They are more tricky to handle than patties because they break or squash more easily and they need turning constantly to brown them all over.

Choose the coating carefully, since a crumb coating may flake or rub off on the grill bars. Flour, oatmeal or other crushed grains are wiser choices.

BEAN AND LENTIL BURGERS

Makes 4 burgers

INGREDIENTS	Metric	Imperial	American
Cooked or canned butter (navy) beans	250 g	9 oz	1½ cups
Cooked red lentils	3 tbsp	3 tbsp	3 tbsp
Margarine	50 g	2 oz	4 tbsp
Large garlic clove, grated (minced)	1	1	1
Medium-sized onion, finely chopped	1	1	1
Milk	300 ml	½ pint	1¼ cups
85% extraction flour	4 tbsp	4 tbsp	4 tbsp
Dried basil	2 tsp	2 tsp	2 tsp
Chopped fresh parsley	2 tbsp	2 tbsp	2 tbsp
Ground coriander	pinch	pinch	pinch
Salt and freshly ground black pepper			
Egg, beaten	2 tbsp	2 tbsp	2 tbsp
Melted margarine for brushing			

Mash or pound the beans and lentils together or purée coarsely in a food processor or blender.

Melt half the margarine in a pan and fry the garlic and onion until soft but not coloured. Warm the milk in a small saucepan.

In another pan, melt the remaining margarine. Stir in the flour and cook for 2 minutes, stirring, without browning. Gradually stir in the warmed milk. Cook over low heat, stirring constantly, until the mixture is very thick. Stir in the fried garlic and onion. Leave until cool enough to handle.

Mix together in a bowl the mashed pulses, garlicky sauce mixture, herbs and coriander and season to taste. Blend in the egg. With floured hands, shape into 4 equal-sized round patties. Chill for 1 hour until firm.

Brush the burgers with melted margarine. Grill (broil) on the barbecue in a double-sided hinged grill or fry on a barbecue griddle pan (page 7). Turn once while grilling or frying. Cook until lightly browned on both sides.

Note: You can add extra herbs or spices to these burgers if you wish.

QUICK CHEESE BEANBURGERS

Makes 6 burgers

INGREDIENTS	Metric	Imperial	American
Canned baked beans in tomato sauce	450 g	15.9 oz	16 oz
Mature Cheddar cheese, grated	75 g	3 oz	¾ cup
Soft wholemeal (whole wheat) breadcrumbs	100 g	4 oz	2 cups
Soy sauce	¼ tsp	¼ tsp	¼ tsp
Egg, beaten	1–2 tbsp	1–2 tbsp	1–2 tbsp
Melted butter or margarine for brushing			

Drain the beans over a small saucepan. Keep the sauce to serve with the burgers. Mash or pound the beans to a coarse paste or process in a food processor. Mix the paste with the cheese, breadcrumbs and soy sauce and bind with the egg. Shape the mixture into 6 flat round patties.

At the barbecue, brush with melted butter or margarine. Cook in a double-sided hinged grill (broiler), turning once, until browned on both sides.

Meanwhile, warm the pan of sauce on the barbecue. Serve with the burgers.

SPLIT PEA PATTIES

Makes 8 patties

INGREDIENTS	Metric	Imperial	American
Split peas	225 g	8 oz	½ lb
Dried onion flakes	2 tbsp	2 tbsp	2 tbsp
Chopped fresh parsley	2 tbsp	2 tbsp	2 tbsp
Dried thyme	1 tsp	1 tsp	1 tsp
Lemon juice	1 tbsp	1 tbsp	1 tbsp
Soy sauce	½ tsp	½ tsp	½ tsp
Egg	1	1	1
Wholemeal (whole wheat) flour as needed	4–6 tbsp	4–6 tbsp	4–6 tbsp
Salt and freshly ground black pepper			
Melted margarine or oil for brushing			
Barbecue Sauce (page 52) or Fresh Tomato Sauce (page 51)			

Boil the split peas in water for 35–45 minutes until tender. Separately, soak the dried onion flakes in a little very hot water for 5 minutes. Drain both the peas and onion flakes thoroughly and cool slightly.

Mash both or process in a food processor with the parsley, thyme, lemon juice, soy sauce and egg until almost smooth. Blend in enough flour to make the mixture easy to mould. Season to taste.

Divide the mixture into 8 equal-sized portions. Shape them into patties about 1 cm/½ inch thick. Dust with flour on both sides.

At the barbecue, brush them with melted margarine or oil. Cook in a Double-Sided grill (page 6) or fry on a barbecue griddle pan (page 7) until browned on both sides.

Serve with Barbecue Sauce or Fresh Tomato Sauce.

SPINACH AND CHEESE CUTLETS

Makes 8 cutlets

INGREDIENTS	*Metric*	*Imperial*	*American*
Finely chopped, cooked fresh spinach, well drained	450 g	1 lb	1 lb
Grated Cheddar cheese	225 g	8 oz	2 cups
Salt and freshly ground black pepper			
Grated nutmeg	pinch	pinch	pinch
Egg yolks	4	4	4
Melted butter or margarine	1 tbsp	1 tbsp	1 tbsp
Dry white breadcrumbs for coating as needed			
Melted butter or margarine for brushing			

Make sure that the spinach is very well drained by squeezing it. Beat into it the cheese, seasoning and nutmeg. Beat 2 of the egg yolks with the 1 tbsp butter or margarine and use to bind the mixture. Chill for 1 hour until firm.

Shape the mixture into 8 equal-sized cutlets. Beat the 2 remaining egg yolks with a little water. Coat the cutlets with egg, then with crumbs, pressing them on firmly. Chill for 30 minutes.

At the barbecue, brush the cutlets with melted fat on both sides. Cook in a double-sided hinged grill (broiler) until lightly browned on both sides. Alternatively cook 3 at a time on a barbecue grill (broiler) tray (page 7) until lightly browned, turning once.

POTATO-CORIANDER PATTIES

Makes 8 patties

INGREDIENTS	Metric	Imperial	American
Potatoes, scrubbed	750 g	1½ lb	1½ lb
Salt			
Split red lentils	50 g	2 oz	¼ cup
Sunflower or corn oil	2 tbsp	2 tbsp	2 tbsp
Cumin seeds	½ tsp	½ tsp	½ tsp
Finely chopped onion	2 tbsp	2 tbsp	2 tbsp
Green coriander leaves, chopped	3 tbsp	3 tbsp	3 tbsp
Ground coriander	¼ tsp	¼ tsp	¼ tsp
Ground cumin	⅛ tsp	⅛ tsp	⅛ tsp
Paprika	⅛ tsp	⅛ tsp	⅛ tsp
Cayenne pepper	⅛ tsp	⅛ tsp	⅛ tsp
Freshly ground black pepper	good pinch	good pinch	good pinch

Flour for dusting
Garlic-flavoured oil for brushing

Boil or bake the potatoes in their skins. Cool until easy to handle. Peel thinly, then mash them with a fork. Add salt to taste and set aside.

Meanwhile, make the filling. Boil the lentils with ½ teaspoon salt until soft. Drain thoroughly.

Heat the 2 tablespoons oil in a frying-pan (skillet) over a low heat. Stir in the cumin seeds. Add the onion and continue stirring for 1 minute. Add the coriander leaves and spices and cook, stirring, for 2 minutes.

Lastly, stir in the red lentils and a good pinch of salt and black pepper. Simmer, stirring frequently, until the mixture is dryish. Leave to cool in the pan.

Shape the mashed potato into a block and cut into 8

equal-sized portions. Roll each into a ball. On a floured surface, flatten the balls into rounds about 5 mm/¼ inch thick.

Divide the filling mixture into 8 equal portions and place one in the centre of each potato round. Press in lightly. Then cover the filling with potato from the edges of the rounds to form patties. Dust lightly with flour and chill for several hours.

To cook, brush with oil. Grill (broil) on the barbecue in a double-sided hinged grill until lightly browned on both sides. Handle carefully as the patties are fragile.

Note: For garlic-flavoured oil, steep a skinned garlic clove in your usual oil for 2–3 days.

CORN ON THE COB Ⓥ

Serves any number

INGREDIENTS	Metric	Imperial	American
Young tender corn on the cob in the husk	1 per person	1 per person	1 per person
Softened butter or margarine	1 tbsp per cob	1 tbsp per cob	1 tbsp per cob

Choose young tender corn which is still pale yellow. Unless the raw kernels dent easily and give out a milky liquid when pressed with a thumbnail, they are elderly and should be parboiled and cooled before being grilled (broiled). See page 89.

Strip back the husk of each cob without detaching it. Pull out the silky 'hair' and discard. Spread the cob with softened butter or margarine. Re-fold the husk leaves over the cob. Insert a short metal skewer in each end of the cob or in the stem end only.

Cook the cobs on the barbecue, turning often with wooden tongs, until the husks begin to char. Strip off the husks and continue cooking the cobs until the kernels begin to bronze. Be careful not to burn them.

Serve on the skewers.

TOASTED BARBECUE SANDWICHES Ⓥ

Makes 8 sandwiches

INGREDIENTS	Metric	Imperial	American
Square slices of wholemeal (whole wheat) bread	16	16	16
Medium-sized firm tomatoes	4	4	4
Soy sauce or Tabasco (hot pepper sauce) for sprinkling			
Salt and freshly ground black pepper			
Peanut butter for spreading	1 tbsp per slice	1 tbsp per slice	1 tbsp per slice
Softened margarine for brushing			

Cut the crusts off the bread slices. Slice the tomatoes into 4 round slices each, discarding the ends. Sprinkle the tomato slices with soy sauce or Tabasco and a little seasoning. Spread one side of each bread slice with peanut butter. Place 2 tomato slices on the buttered sides of 8 slices. Cover with the remaining slices, buttered side down. Press the sandwiches to 'seal' them. Brush lightly with margarine on both sides. Place in a double-sided hinged grill (broiler) and toast, turning once, until lightly browned on both sides.

As an alternative filling, use one of the following: mashed cooked carrot or green peas, mixed with a little finely shredded lettuce and the same seasoning; mashed cooked lentils and finely chopped walnuts with the same seasoning.

If you eat dairy foods, use one of the following: grated Cheddar cheese mixed with the same seasoning; soft scrambled egg mixed with the same seasoning; cottage cheese with chives, mixed with the same seasoning.

CHEESY-TOPPED TOMATOES

INGREDIENTS	Metric	Imperial	American
Medium-sized tomatoes	8	8	8
Salad oil			
Medium-sized onion, finely chopped	1	1	1
Finely chopped fresh parsley	4 tbsp	4 tbsp	4 tbsp
Soft wholemeal (whole wheat) breadcrumbs	75 g	3 oz	1½ cups
Salt and freshly ground black pepper			
Small thin squares of cheese	16	16	16

Cut the tomatoes in half across and scoop out the seeds. Brush the insides with oil. Mix the onion with the parsley and breadcrumbs and season to taste. Use to stuff the tomato halves.

Place on an oiled barbecue tray 10–15cm/4–6 inches above the cooler coals and cook for about 5 minutes. Top each tomato half with a square of cheese and cook for a further 5 minutes.

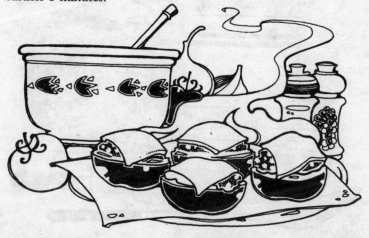

TRIPLE WINNERS Ⓥ

Enough vegetables to fill one 'net' (page 6)

INGREDIENTS	Metric	Imperial	American
Cauliflower florets, fairly large	100 g	4 oz	¼ lb
Medium-thin carrot, cut into 3 cm/1 inch pieces	75 g	3 oz	3 oz
Green pepper, de-seeded and cut into 4 pieces	½	½	½
Salt			
Garlic Marinade and Baste (page 50)			

Cook all the vegetables in boiling salted water for 5–7 minutes or until just tender. Drain well. While still hot soak them in the Garlic Marinade and Baste until you are ready to grill (broil) them.

With a slotted spoon, pack the vegetables into a vegetable 'net'. Grill on the barbecue, turning the 'net' over 2 or 3 times and basting with more Garlic Marinade and Baste.

They are ready to eat when just crisp and lightly browned.

PARSNIP-PEPPER KEBABS Ⓥ

INGREDIENTS	Metric	Imperial	American
Red pepper, de-seeded and cut into 8 squares	1	1	1
Yellow pepper, de-seeded and cut into 8 squares	1	1	1
Green pepper, de-seeded and cut into 8 squares	1	1	1
Pickling (baby) onions, peeled	8	8	8
Slices of courgette (zucchini), 3 cm/1½ inches thick	8	8	8
Cubes of cooked parsnip, 4 cm/1½ inches thick	8	8	8
Soy Dressing (page 41)			

Soak 4 30 cm/12 inch wooden skewers in water for 1 hour.

Meanwhile, cook the pepper squares in boiling water until tender. Drain and cool. Cook the onions in boiling water until tender. Drain and cool. Blanch the courgette slices in boiling water for 4 minutes. Drain and cool.

On each skewer thread a piece of red pepper, then a parsnip cube, a piece of yellow pepper, an onion, a piece of green pepper and a slice of courgette. Repeat the process, using all of the ingredients.

At the barbecue, brush the kebabs well with Soy Dressing and grill (broil) over medium heat, turning 2 or 3 times until the kebabs are hot and glazed. Baste when turning.

FOUR SEASONS KEBABS Ⓥ

INGREDIENTS	Metric	Imperial	American
Small firm Brussels sprouts, fresh or frozen	12	12	12
Large red pepper, de-seeded and cut into 8 squares	1	1	1
Thin round slices of raw carrot	4	4	4
New or frozen new potatoes	4	4	4
Medium-sized button mushrooms, stems removed	4	4	4
Herb Baste for Vegetables (page 53)			
Yellow Rice (page 82)			

Ahead of time, soak 4 30 cm/12 inch wooden skewers in water for 1 hour.

Bring a pan of water to the boil. Add the Brussels sprouts and squares of pepper and cook for 5–6 minutes or until just tender. Add the carrot slices after 1 minute. Add the potatoes for only just long enough to cook them through; they should still be firm. Frozen potatoes should only need 1–2 minutes' cooking.

Drain all the vegetables and cool until easy to handle. Brush the mushroom caps well all over with Herb Baste.

On each soaked skewer, thread first a Brussels sprout, followed by a piece of pepper, then a potato. Next add a carrot slice, then another sprout. Add a mushroom, a second piece of pepper, and lastly a third sprout.

At the barbecue, brush the kebabs all over with Herb Baste. Cook on the barbecue grill (broiler rack), turning often, until sprouts and potatoes are touched with brown. Brush with baste two or three times while cooking.

Serve with Yellow Rice.

'SAUSAGE' AND CHEESE KEBABS

INGREDIENTS	Metric	Imperial	American
Pieces of firm commercial soya 'sausage' 3 cm/ 1 inch long (see note)	8	8	8
Wine Marinade for Vegetables (page 49)			
Large button mushrooms, stems removed	8	8	8
Soy Marinade for Bean Curd (page 48)			
Red peppers, de-seeded and cut into 8 pieces	2	2	2
Mozzarella cheese, cut into 8 stubby 'sticks'	50 g	2 oz	2 oz
Oil for brushing			

Marinate the pieces of soya 'sausage' in the Wine Marinade and the mushroom caps in the Soy Marinade overnight.

Soak 4 30 cm/12 inch wooden skewers in water for 1 hour. Cook the pepper pieces in boiling water until tender. Drain and cool.

Thread a piece of soya 'sausage' onto each skewer. Wrap a cheese 'stick' in a piece of pepper, enclosing it completely, and impale on each skewer. Add a mushroom cap to each skewer. Repeat the process, using all the ingredients.

At the barbecue, brush the pepper pieces lightly with oil if you wish. Cook on the barbecue grill (broiler rack), turning once or twice, until the 'sausage' pieces are slightly coloured and the mushrooms are sizzling. Baste with a little oil if needed while cooking.

Serve with Spinach Pasta (page 83).

Note: Commercial soya 'sausages' vary a good deal. Choose a light-coloured type, about 2 cm/¾ inch in diameter. Skin it if required before cutting up and marinating.

HERB AND NUT KOFTA

(Vegetarian 'meatballs')

Makes about 24 'meatballs'

INGREDIENTS	Metric	Imperial	American
Skimmed (skim) milk or soya milk	275 ml	½ pint	1¼ cups
Cornmeal or semolina	50 g	2 oz	⅓ cup
Salt	¼ tsp	¼ tsp	¼ tsp
Black pepper	pinch	pinch	pinch
Mixed spice	pinch	pinch	pinch
Finely chopped fresh herbs (see note)	½ tbsp	½ tbsp	½ tbsp
White or wholemeal (whole wheat) flour	50 g	2 oz	½ cup
Egg, beaten	1	1	1
Mixed chopped nuts	50 g	2 oz	⅓ cup
Melted butter or margarine for brushing			

Bring the milk to the boil in a medium-sized saucepan. Stir in the cornmeal or semolina and season lightly. Reduce the heat and simmer, stirring constantly, until the mixture is very thick. Remove from the heat and gradually stir in all the other ingredients except the melted butter or margarine. Blend thoroughly. Cool, then chill for 30 minutes.

With floured hands, roll teaspoonfuls of mixture into small balls about 3 cm/1 inch across. Thread on well-soaked wooden skewers and brush with melted butter or margarine. Grill (broil) on the barbecue, turning 2 or 3 times, until exposed surfaces are browned and the kofta are hot. Alternatively, shallow fry a few at a time in a small heavy frying pan (skillet), shaking the pan until the balls are lightly browned.

Note: Fresh thyme and parsley should be obtainable in winter. (A pot of thyme is a super kitchen standby.) If no fresh herbs are available, use 1 generous teaspoon newly bought dried herbs such as thyme and rosemary.

MUSHROOM KEBABS Ⓥ

INGREDIENTS	Metric	Imperial	American
Large button mushrooms, stems removed	16	16	16
Small red peppers, de-seeded and cut into 6 pieces	2	2	2
Large courgette, topped and tailed and cut into 12 slices	1	1	1
Medium-sized firm yellow banana, peeled and cut into 12 slices, just before use	1	1	1
Salt and white pepper			
Melted butter or oil for brushing			

Thread the mushroom caps, pepper pieces, courgette and banana slices onto 4 skewers, beginning and ending with a mushroom.

Season on all sides and brush with melted butter or oil. Cook near the edge of the barbecue, turning frequently, until the pepper and courgette are tender.

The discarded mushroom stems can be used to flavour soup or a casserole.

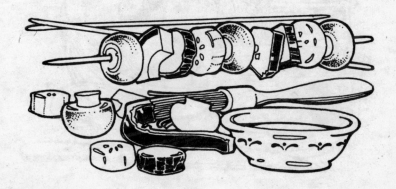

SWEET FRUIT KEBABS

Any firm fruit makes delicious sweet kebabs if you want to offer a barbecued hot dessert. Pineapple, apple or pear cubes, apricot halves (fresh or canned), banana chunks, quartered kiwi fruit or plums and whole large strawberries can all be grilled.

Remember that many fruits discolour when peeled or cut up, so it is wise to macerate any fruit from the moment you prepare it until you thread it on skewers for barbecuing. Soak it in wine or fruit juice, perhaps 'laced' with a little liqueur; a minature bottle does not cost much. Use melted butter, margarine or a light oil for brushing and basting.

BARBECUE 'FRY-UPS' AND STIR-FRIES

BARBECUE BRUNCH FRY-UP

Serves 1

INGREDIENTS	Metric	Imperial	American
Egg	1	1	1
Salt and freshly ground black pepper			
Tomato, sliced	1	1	1
Wholemeal (whole wheat) flour for dusting			
Split Pea Patty (page 58)	1	1	1
Corn or other light oil for frying			

Crack the egg into a cup without breaking the yolk. Season the tomato slices on both sides and dust with flour. Dust the patty with a little flour if at all damp.

Film a barbecue griddle pan with oil and heat it on the barbecue grill (broiler rack). Using a metal spatula, lay the tomato slices in the large compartment and the patty in one small compartment. Cook for 1–3 minutes until the patty is brown underneath. Turn it over and slip the egg into the second small compartment. Cook until the egg is just set.

Remove the food to a plate with the spatula and season it to taste.

BARBECUED OMELETTE

Serves 1

INGREDIENTS	Metric	Imperial	American
Eggs, well beaten	2	2	2
Salt and white pepper			
Butter or margarine	1 tsp	1 tsp	1 tsp

Heat a small omelette pan (about 15 cm/6 inches) on the barbecue grill. When hot, add the fat and swirl it round in the pan as it melts, so that it films the base.

Pour in the eggs, swirling the pan to spread them all over. Cook on the grill, shaking the pan slightly and loosening the edges of the omelette with a pliable palette knife (metal spatula), until the eggs are set underneath and the top is just moist. With the palette knife, fold one half of the omelette over the other half. Slide the omelette out of the pan onto a warm plate.

Any usual omelette fillings can be served in a barbecued omelette. Marinated Tofu (page 26) is particularly good.

POTATO CAKES Ⓥ

Makes 6 'cakes'

INGREDIENTS	Metric	Imperial	American
Hot mashed potato, freshly made	350 g	12 oz	1¼ cups
Salt and white pepper			
Dijon mustard	¼ tsp	¼ tsp	¼ tsp
Chopped fresh parsley	2 tsp	2 tsp	2 tsp
Wholemeal (whole wheat) flour	3 tbsp	3 tbsp	3 tbsp
Celery seeds	½ tsp	½ tsp	½ tsp
Oil			

Season the mashed potato well with salt and pepper. Blend in the mustard. Mix in the parsley with a fork. Cool the potato completely.

Season the flour with salt and pepper and mix in the celery seeds. Spread the flour on a piece of greaseproof (waxed) paper. Shape the potato mixture into 6 equal-sized small patties, and coat them with flour.

Film a frying pan (skillet) or a barbecue griddle pan (page 7) with oil and heat on the barbecue. Fry the patties, turning once, until browned on both sides.

FRIED SNACKS Ⓥ

De-seeded rings of unpeeled green pepper make excellent 'nibbles' when lightly fried on a Barbecue Griddle Pan or in a frying pan (skillet) on the barbecue grill rack. Cut the rings about 5 mm/¼ inch thick and pat them dry to prevent spitting. Season very lightly with salt and black pepper and fry on the cooler coals, turning once.

Whole button mushrooms sliced lengthways are similar goodies. Trim the ends of the stems neatly before slicing. Sprinkle the slices lightly with vinegar and season well. Fry, turning once, until lightly browned on both sides.

Both these tempting titbits are good additions to a mixed vegetable 'fry-up'.

SUPER CURRIED STIR-FRY Ⓥ

INGREDIENTS	Metric	Imperial	American
Coconut milk (see method)	300 ml	½ pint	1¼ cups
Potatoes, peeled and cut into 2 cm/¾ inch cubes	225 g	8 oz	1⅓ cups
White cabbage without coarse ribs, finely shredded	75 g	3 oz	1 cup
Shelled peas, fresh or frozen	100 g	4 oz	¾ cup
Medium-sized carrots, thinly sliced	100 g	4 oz	1 cup
Oil	3 tbsp	3 tbsp	3 tbsp
Medium-sized onions, thinly sliced	2	2	2
Garlic clove, grated (minced)	¼	¼	¼
Green pepper, de-seeded and cut into 'matchsticks'	½	½	½
Spices mixed in a bowl			
Ground coriander	2 tsp	2 tsp	2 tsp
Ground cumin	¼ tsp	¼ tsp	¼ tsp
Chilli (chili) powder	⅓ tsp	⅓ tsp	⅓ tsp
Ground ginger	¼ tsp	¼ tsp	¼ tsp
Turmeric	¼ tsp	¼ tsp	¼ tsp
Salt	¼–½ tsp	¼–½ tsp	¼–½ tsp
Ground cinnamon	pinch	pinch	pinch
Ground cloves	pinch	pinch	pinch
Lemon juice	2 tsp	2 tsp	2 tsp

Make the coconut milk ahead of time. Pour 300 ml/½ pint/1¼ cups boiling water over 100 g/4 oz/1⅓ cups desiccated (shredded) coconut. Leave (let stand) for 2 hours. Process both coconut and liquid in an electric blender. Strain through a very fine sieve. Squeeze the remaining coconut to extract as much liquid as possible. Pour into a jug.

In the kitchen, gently cook the potato, cabbage, peas and carrots in boiling water for 5 minutes. Drain and place in a bowl. Take all the ingredients to the barbecue.

On the barbecue, heat the oil in a wok or deep frying pan (skillet). Stir the onions and garlic in the oil until golden. Add the green pepper and spice mixture and stir round. Add the cooked vegetables and stir in. Cook over medium-hot coals for 4 minutes, stirring twice.

Add the coconut milk and lemon juice, move the pan to the side of the barbecue and cook gently until all the vegetables are crisp-tender and the whole dish is well heated.

SPICY SLICES Ⓥ

INGREDIENTS	Metric	Imperial	American
Cornflour (cornstarch)	4 tbsp	4 tbsp	4 tbsp
Chilli (chili) powder	1/8 tsp	1/8 tsp	1/8 tsp
Ground cumin	1/8 tsp	1/8 tsp	1/8 tsp
Paprika	1/8 tsp	1/8 tsp	1/8 tsp
Turmeric	1/8 tsp	1/8 tsp	1/8 tsp
Large courgettes (zucchini), about 150g/5 oz each, cut into 5 mm/1/4 inch rounds	2	2	2
Salt and black pepper			
Oil			

Mix together the cornflour and spices on a plate. Coat both sides of the courgette slices with the mixture, pressing it on firmly. Season to taste.

Film a frying pan or a barbecue griddle pan (page 7) with oil. Fry the slices, a few at a time, until slightly softened and lightly browned on both sides. Drain on absorbent kitchen paper while frying the remaining slices.

Fry peeled aubergine (eggplant) slices the same way. Use the same quantities of coating ingredients to fry slices of one medium-sized aubergine, about 400 g/14 oz in weight.

Serve as a side dish or as part of a mixed 'fry-up'.

MEXICAN REFRIED BEANS

(Frijoles refritos)

This is a modern version of an old, ever-popular Mexican Indian recipe. Like Mexican cooks, you can vary the quantities of the flavourings and oil to suit your own taste.

INGREDIENTS	Metric	Imperial	American
Cans of chilli (chili) beans (415 g/14½ oz each)	2 cans	2 cans	2 cans
Salt and freshly ground black pepper			
Finely chopped onion	3 tbsp	3 tbsp	3 tbsp
Oregano	2 tsp	2 tsp	2 tsp
Oil for first frying	4 tbsp	4 tbsp	4 tbsp
Extra oil for re-frying	2–3 tbsp	2–3 tbsp	2–3 tbsp

Drain the beans over a jug and reserve the liquid. Crush or chop the beans roughly by pounding or in a food processor. Season well and mix in the onion and oregano.

In the kitchen, heat the 4 tablespoons oil in a frying pan (skillet). Add about one third of the beans and mash them in the hot fat with a wooden spoon until they are pasty. Stir in a little of the reserved liquid. When well blended, add more beans. Mash them down, then stir in a little more liquid. Repeat the process once or twice, using all the beans and about half the liquid. Simmer gently, stirring frequently, until the pasty mixture leaves the bottom of the pan clean when a spoon is drawn across it. Turn the mixture into a bowl, cover and transfer to the Cook's Table at the barbecue.

At the barbecue, heat the extra oil in a frying pan over medium-hot coals. Add the mashed bean paste, pressing it down to spread it out. Fry, stirring gently, until the paste has crisp brown patches underneath. Turn it over with a palette knife (metal spatula) to fry the top surface.

Note: If you want a milder, but less Mexican flavour, substitute plain red kidney beans for the chilli beans.

SPECTRUM STIR-FRY Ⓥ

INGREDIENTS	Metric	Imperial	American
Medium-sized leek, green and white parts, thoroughly washed and sliced into rings	1	1	1
Can of sweetcorn (whole kernel corn) with peppers, drained (198 g/7 oz)	198 g	7 oz	8 oz
Cooked or well-drained, canned red kidney beans (213 g/7½ oz can)	125 g	4 oz	4 oz
Medium-sized carrot, coarsely chopped	1	1	1
Spring onions (scallions), green and white parts, coarsely chopped	4	4	4
Celery sticks (stalks) coarsely chopped,	2	2	2
Sherry	1 tbsp	1 tbsp	1 tbsp
Soy sauce	1 tbsp	1 tbsp	1 tbsp
Tomato juice	1 tbsp	1 tbsp	1 tbsp
Water	1 tbsp	1 tbsp	1 tbsp
Oil	3 tbsp	3 tbsp	3 tbsp

In the kitchen, cook the leek in a little boiling water for 5 minutes. Drain. Place in a bowl with the corn and beans. Place the carrot, spring onions and celery in a second bowl. Stir the sherry, soy sauce, tomato juice and water in a jug. Take to the barbecue.

On the barbecue, heat the oil in a wok or deep frying pan (skillet). Add the carrots, onions and celery and stir over medium-hot coals for 3 minutes. Add the leek, sweetcorn and beans and stir for a further 3–4 minutes. Add the liquid from the jug, cover the pan and simmer, without stirring, for 3 minutes or until all the liquid is absorbed.

BARBECUED SALAD STIR-FRY Ⓥ

All the cooking can be done on the barbecue if you have space for the pan.

INGREDIENTS	Metric	Imperial	American
Oil	3 tbsp	3 tbsp	3 tbsp
Green pepper, de-seeded and finely chopped	1	1	1
Medium-sized leeks, thoroughly washed and sliced into thin rings	2	2	2
Large garlic clove, squeezed through a press over leeks	1	1	1
Button mushrooms, sliced	100 g	4 oz	1 cup
Tomatoes, chopped	225 g	8 oz	1 cup
Cucumber, quartered lengthways and sliced into thin fans	100 g	4 oz	1 cup
Bean sprouts	175 g	6 oz	3 cups
Salt and black pepper			
Strong vegetable stock	2 tbsp	2 tbsp	2 tbsp
Sherry	1 tbsp	1 tbsp	1 tbsp

Heat 2 tablespoons of the oil in a wok or deep frying-pan (skillet) and stir-fry the green pepper, leek rings and garlic for 3 minutes. Add the mushrooms, tomatoes and any free juice, with the remaining oil. Stir for another 2 minutes. Stir in the cucumber and bean sprouts, seasoning to taste, stock and sherry. Stir until the sprouts soften.

Cover the pan and leave to steam for 3–4 minutes, to soften the cucumber and blend the flavours. Do not over-cook. Adjust the seasoning before serving.

CALABRESE STIR-FRY

Fry on the barbecue if this is your main dish or if you have space for it as well as others. Alternatively, just transfer it to the barbecue for simmering.

INGREDIENTS	Metric	Imperial	American
Calabrese florets with 3 cm/1 inch stems	350 g	12 oz	¾ lb
Sweet potato or parsnip, peeled and cut into 2 cm/¾ inch cubes	225 g	8 oz	½ lb
Salt			
Medium-sized onion, finely sliced	1	1	1
Oil	2 tbsp	2 tbsp	2 tbsp
Medium-sized tomatoes, thinly sliced	3	3	3
Medium-sized courgettes (zucchini), coarsely grated	2	2	2
Dried thyme	½ tbsp	½ tbsp	½ tbsp
Vegetable stock	2–4 tbsp	2–4 tbsp	2–4 tbsp
Sherry (optional)	2 tbsp	2 tbsp	2 tbsp
Salt and black pepper			

In the kitchen, parboil the calabrese florets and the potato or parsnip cubes in boiling salted water for 5 minutes. Drain and mix with the onion.

Heat the oil in a wok or deep frying-pan. This can be done on the barbecue if you wish. Add the mixed vegetables and stir with a wooden spoon for 4 minutes. Add the tomato slices and courgettes and stir for another 3 minutes. Sprinkle with thyme, 2 tablespoons stock, sherry if using it and seasoning to taste.

Transfer to the barbecue if fried in the kitchen. Cover the pan, reheat and simmer for 4 minutes, adding the extra stock if required to prevent the stir-fry from drying out.

Note: Calabrese florets tend to break up when stir-fried, making the dish attractively speckled with green.

BARBECUE 'SIMMERERS'

All the following dishes, except pasta, can be cooked on a barbecue almost 'from scratch', given time, space and care. However do practise before you try them out on guests to make sure that your pans are suitable and easy to manage; also that there is enough space for them when other items are being cooked. Do any initial frying and bring liquids to the boil on the kitchen cooker before transferring the pans to the barbecue. Time the cooking from when the pan returns to the boil.

Both rice and pasta, kept warm in a colander, will need to be forked over before serving, to separate the grains or strands.

BULGHAR Ⓥ
(to use instead of rice)

Bulghar is a partly cooked and dried form of cracked wheat, available in most Health Food stores. It is almost foolproof to cook and makes a delicious nutty alternative to rice or pasta. It is particularly suitable for barbecuing because, after heating, it only needs to simmer gently.

For 4 people, place 175 g/6 oz/1 cup dry bulghar in a heavy saucepan with a heat-resistant handle. In the kitchen shake the pan gently over medium-high heat for 3 minutes. Pour on 450 ml/¾ pint/2 cups water and stir round. Bring to the boil.

Cover the pan and transfer to the barbecue quickly. Simmer the bulghar, covered, for 20 minutes, stirring occasionally, to prevent it from sticking. Season to taste and leave at the side of the barbecue until you want to serve it.

SPICED BULGHAR WITH PINE NUTS Ⓥ

INGREDIENTS	Metric	Imperial	American
Oil	4 tbsp	4 tbsp	4 tbsp
Onions, finely chopped	225 g	8 oz	½ lb
Garlic clove, finely chopped	½	½	½
Pine nut kernels	2 tbsp	2 tbsp	2 tbsp
Bulghar	150 g	5 oz	scant 1 cup
Salt and freshly ground black pepper			
Vegetable stock	600 ml	1 pint	2½ cups
Seedless raisins	2 tbsp	2 tbsp	2 tbsp
Ground coriander	¼ tsp	¼ tsp	¼ tsp
Ground cinnamon	¼ tsp	¼ tsp	¼ tsp

Heat half the oil in a heavy pan with a heat-resistant handle and sauté the onion, garlic and pine nuts until the onion is soft. Stir in the bulghar and remaining oil and stir for 3 minutes. Season well. Stir in the stock and the remaining ingredients. Cover the pan and bring to the boil.

Transfer to the barbecue and simmer, covered, for 15–20 minutes or until all the stock is absorbed. Transfer to the side of the barbecue. Keep warm for 25–30 minutes before serving, to let the bulghar become soft and swollen.

Note: This makes an excellent salad served cold.

BROWN RICE Ⓥ

INGREDIENTS	Metric	Imperial	American
Brown rice (any type)	225 g	8 oz	generous 1 cup
Water as needed			
Oil	2 tsp	2 tsp	2 tsp
Salt			

Rinse the rice in a colander under cold running water. Place in a heavy pan with a stout heat-resistant handle. Add enough water to cover the rice with 8 cm/3 inches clear water above. Add the oil. Bring to the boil. Transfer to the barbecue if you wish.

Cover the pan and simmer for 40–45 minutes or until the rice is tender but still chewy. Towards the end, check that it is not drying out and add a little boiling water if necessary. Drain off any remaining water when the rice is ready. Add salt to taste and keep the rice hot in a cloth-lined colander over a pan of simmering water on the barbecue or in a heat-resistant dish on a warming shelf or hot-plate.

YELLOW RICE Ⓥ

INGREDIENTS	Metric	Imperial	American
Water	750 ml	1¼ pints	3 cups
Long grain rice	200 g	7 oz	1 cup
Cinnamon stick	1	1	1
Turmeric	½ tsp	½ tsp	½ tsp
Salt	1 tsp	1 tsp	1 tsp
Butter or margarine	1 tbsp	1 tbsp	1 tbsp
Seedless raisins (optional)	75 g	3 oz	½ cup

In the kitchen, bring the water to the boil in a large saucepan. Sprinkle in the rice. Add all the other ingredients and stir round once. Bring back to the boil. Transfer to the barbecue if you wish.

Cook until the rice is tender and has absorbed all the water. Add a little more boiling water if the rice looks like drying out, but do not let it become soggy. Turn the hot cooked rice into a cloth-lined colander and keep it warm over a pan of simmering water on the barbecue or as suggested for Brown Rice (opposite). Cover the pan until ready to serve.

WHOLEMEAL (WHOLE WHEAT) AND SPINACH PASTA

The easiest pasta to use for serving with barbecued foods is fresh or dried 'instant' pasta which cooks in 4 minutes or less in boiling water. However, like other dried pasta, it needs plenty of fast-boiling water which is not easy to provide on the barbecue. Any pasta is therefore best cooked in the kitchen, ahead of time if you prefer. It can then be kept warm or reheated in a cloth-lined colander over a little simmering water on the barbecue.

Ordinary (regular) dried pasta takes from 5–20 minutes to cook, depending on size. Allow about 75 g/3 oz/scant 1 cup pasta per person and choose 'nests' or coils of thin pasta or elbow cut pasta rather than long rods. Drop the pasta shapes into the fast-boiling water a few at a time so that the water does not go off the boil. Cook until the pasta is 'al dente' and has no floury taste left. Test whether it is done by nibbling a piece from time to time. Be careful not to overcook it. Drain, transfer to the barbecue and keep warm until required.

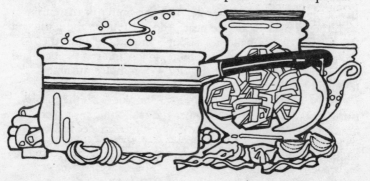

RATATOUILLE Ⓥ

INGREDIENTS	Metric	Imperial	American
Butter or margarine	25 g	1 oz	2 tbsp
Olive oil	3 tbsp	3 tbsp	3 tbsp
Large onions, thinly sliced	2	2	2
Garlic cloves, crushed	2	2	2
Medium-sized aubergines (eggplants), thinly sliced	3	3	3
Large green pepper, de-seeded and chopped	1	1	1
Large red pepper, de-seeded and chopped	1	1	1
Medium-sized courgettes (zucchini), sliced	5	5	5
Can of tomatoes (397 g/14 oz)	1 can	1 can	1 can
Dried basil	1 tsp	1 tsp	1 tsp
Dried rosemary	1 tsp	1 tsp	1 tsp
Bay leaves	2	2	2
Salt	1½ tsp	1½ tsp	1½ tsp
Freshly ground black pepper	¾ tsp	¾ tsp	¾ tsp
Chopped fresh parsley	2 tbsp	2 tbsp	2 tbsp

In a large flameproof casserole, melt the butter or margarine with the oil over moderate heat. Add the onions and garlic and fry, stirring occasionally, for about 5 minutes or until the onions are soft. Add the aubergine, green and red peppers and courgettes to the casserole. Fry for 4–5 minutes, turning frequently. Add the tomatoes and their juice, the basil, rosemary, bay leaves and seasoning. Sprinkle with the parsley. Bring to the boil. Cover. Simmer the ratatouille over medium heat for 40–50 minutes until the vegetables are cooked.

Keep the casserole hot at the side of the barbecue until ready to serve. Ideal with pasta and barbecued burgers.

FOIL-WRAPPED BARBECUE 'BAKES'

Foil-wrapping is one of the simplest ways to prepare vegetables and fruit for barbecuing. You can choose from several different seasonings and various garnishes. Some ideas are suggested in the recipes below.

Wash any vegetable well, but do not dry it; the extra moisture is enough to steam-cook most vegetables. Wrap tightly in heavy-duty foil, then place on the barbecue grill rack 10–15cm/4–6 inches above the coals. Use wooden barbecue tongs for turning the foil packages when required.

GREEN PEAS AND MUSHROOMS Ⓥ

INGREDIENTS	Metric	Imperial	American
Green peas in pods	900 g	2 lb	2 lb
Mushrooms, thinly sliced	25 g	1 oz	¼ cup
Salt and freshly ground black pepper			
Butter or margarine	2 tbsp	2 tbsp	2 tbsp

Shell the peas, rinse well and place on heavy-duty foil. Scatter the mushrooms on top, season to taste and dot with butter or margarine. Wrap tightly and place on the barbecue 10–15 cm/4–6 inches above medium-hot coals. Cook, turning the package over occasionally, for about 20 minutes.

GREEN BEANS WITH ALMONDS Ⓥ

INGREDIENTS	Metric	Imperial	American
Green beans	450 g	1 lb	1 lb
Salt and white pepper			
Fresh or dried savory leaves	1 tsp	1 tsp	1 tsp
Butter or margarine	2 tbsp	2 tbsp	2 tbsp
Toasted flaked almonds	2 tbsp	2 tbsp	2 tbsp

Top and tail the beans and string if required. Wash and place on heavy-duty foil. Add salt and pepper to taste and sprinkle with savory. Dot with butter or margarine. Wrap tightly, and place on the barbecue 10–15 cm/4–6 inches above medium-hot coals. Cook, turning the package over occasionally, for about 20 minutes or until the beans are as cooked as you like them when pierced with a skewer.

Just before serving, sprinkle with the almonds.

STANDBY POTATOES Ⓥ

Serves any number

INGREDIENTS

Large equal-sized baking potatoes without 'eyes'
Oil for greasing

Choice of fillings
Grated cheese, soured (sour) cream, Herb Baste (page 53), Green Onion Dressing (page 40) or a soft cheese

Cut out squares of foil which will each enclose a potato completely. Brush them well with oil. Prick the potatoes with a fork all over. Make a cross-cut in the skin on one side of each potato. Wrap each potato in a square of foil, cut side up, twisting the edges of the foil together over the top to make a knot. Bake at 200°C/400°F/Gas Mark 6 for 1 hour or until almost tender when pierced with a skewer through the foil. The exact time will depend on the size of the potatoes.

Transfer the wrapped potatoes to the barbecue, foil knots upwards, placing them near the edge. Complete their cooking. When ready to serve, open up the foil, fold back the cross-cut flaps of skin and fill each potato with 1–2 tbsp of your chosen filling.

Baked potatoes are a wonderful standby in case 'rain stops play'. You can complete the cooking in the oven and give everyone a hot filling dish with the salads and desserts you have prepared, even if you cannot cook all the grills indoors.

CARROTS Ⓥ

INGREDIENTS	Metric	Imperial	American
Small carrots, well rinsed and cut into 3 cm/1 inch pieces	450 g	1 lb	1 lb
Salt and freshly ground black pepper			
Butter or margarine	2 tbsp	2 tbsp	2 tbsp
Grated lemon rind (zest)	1 tbsp	1 tbsp	1 tbsp

Place the carrots on heavy-duty foil. Add salt and pepper to taste and dot with the butter or margarine. Sprinkle the lemon rind over. Wrap tightly and place on the barbecue 10–15 cm/4–6 inches above medium-hot coals. Cook, turning over occasionally, for 20–25 minutes.

Treat 3 cm/1 inch lengths of celery stalk in the same way, but use Herb Baste (page 53) instead of plain butter or margarine and omit the lemon rind.

PITTA PACKETS Ⓥ

Makes 8 packets

INGREDIENTS	Metric	Imperial	American
Leeks (white stems), thoroughly washed and sliced into thin rounds	225 g	8 oz	½ lb
Vegetable stock	300 ml	½ pint	1¼ cups
Small apple, chopped	1	1	1
Red radishes, topped and tailed and chopped	6	6	6
Button mushrooms, finely sliced	4	4	4
Grated fresh ginger root	2 tsp	2 tsp	2 tsp
Salt and freshly ground black pepper			
French Dressing (page 39)			
Wholemeal (whole wheat) pitta breads	4	4	4
Softened margarine for brushing			

Cook the leeks in the stock until just tender. Drain and cool. Mix together the drained leeks, apple, radishes, mushrooms and ginger in a bowl. Season well and sprinkle with a little dressing.

Wrap the pitta breads in foil and warm them in the oven for a few moments to soften. Cut them in half across. Stuff them three quarters full with the salad mixture. Brush the outsides of the breads with margarine.

At the barbecue, wrap each packet separately in foil and heat over medium-hot coals for 5–6 minutes, turning once.

FOIL-WRAPPED CORN ON THE COB Ⓥ

Ripe yellow corn with tough kernels is usually best parboiled, then 'baked' in foil on the barbecue. Frozen corn cobs are sold without husks and should therefore also be 'baked' in foil, to prevent them from drying out and charring before they are tender.

INGREDIENTS	Metric	Imperial	American
Ripe or thawed frozen corn cobs	4	4	4
Softened butter or margarine	4 tbsp	4 tbsp	4 tbsp
Salt and black pepper			

Remove the husks and silky 'hair' of elderly corn. Place the husks in the bottom of a pan which will hold the cobs. Lay the cobs on the husks, cover with boiling water and cook for 5–8 minutes until the kernels lift off fairly easily.

Place each cob on a square of foil spread with softened butter or margarine and sprinkle with salt and pepper to taste. Fold the foil squares round the cobs to make parcels. Cook on the barbecue 10–15 cm/4–6 inches above medium-hot coals, turning the packages over often, until the cobs are well heated through and the kernels lift off readily.

COVERED TOMATO PARCEL Ⓥ

INGREDIENTS	Metric	Imperial	American
Medium-sized courgettes (zucchini), cut into 1 cm/½ inch rounds	2	2	2
Medium-sized tomatoes, skinned and cut into wedges	2	2	2
Medium-sized onion, thinly sliced	1	1	1
Salt and freshly ground black pepper			
Oregano	½ tsp	½ tsp	½ tsp
Olive oil or salad oil	1 tbsp	1 tbsp	1 tbsp

Pile half the courgette rounds, tomato wedges and onion together in an even layer on heavy-duty foil. Add salt and pepper to taste and sprinkle with ¼ teaspoon oregano. Pile the remaining vegetables on top of the first layer. Season again and sprinkle with remaining oregano. Pour the oil over the vegetables.

Seal tightly in the foil and place on the barbecue 10–15 cm/4–6 inches above medium-hot coals. Cook, turning the package over occasionally, for 25–30 minutes or until the vegetables are as cooked as you like them when pierced with a skewer.

FOIL-BAKED ONIONS

Serves any number

INGREDIENTS

**Large onions about 350 g/
   12 oz/¾ lb each
Oil for greasing**

Choice of fillings
**Soured (sour) cream, any
   soft cheese or Yogurt
   Dressing (page 40)**

Cut out squares of foil which will each enclose an onion
completely. Brush well with oil. Cut off the roots of the onions
but do not skin them. Cut a deep cross in the top of each
onion, almost down to the centre. Place one onion in the
middle of each foil square and lift the foil around it, twisting it
into a knot over the top of the onion. Bake the onions at
180°C/350°F/Gas Mark 4 for about 1 hour until nearly cooked.

Transfer to the barbecue and complete the cooking over
the coals at the edge of the fire. When ready, place each
onion on a plate, open the foil and fold back the cross-cut
flaps of brown skin. Open out the cut onion flesh with a small
spoon and put in 1 tablespoon of your chosen filling. Eat with
a fork.

APPLES Ⓥ

INGREDIENTS	Metric	Imperial	American
Medium-sized apples	4	4	4
Lemon juice	2 tsp	2 tsp	2 tsp
Butter or margarine	2 tbsp	2 tbsp	2 tbsp
Sugar	1 tbsp	1 tbsp	1 tbsp
Ground cinnamon or coriander			

Wash the apples and peel them if you wish, then slice them. Lay them on a large sheet of heavy-duty foil in one layer. Sprinkle them with the lemon juice and dot with butter or margarine. Sprinkle with sugar and your chosen spice to taste. Wrap closely in the foil.

Place the package on the barbecue 10–15 cm/4–6 inches above hot or medium-hot coals. Cook, moving the package to a new spot occasionally, for 12–15 minutes or until the fruit is well heated through.

Serve as a dessert with a dollop of sweetened whipped cream or soured (sour) cream.

SPICED BANANAS Ⓥ

INGREDIENTS	Metric	Imperial	American
Medium-sized bananas	4	4	4
Butter or margarine	1 tbsp	1 tbsp	1 tbsp
Sugar	1 tsp	1 tsp	1 tsp
Ground cinnamon	1 tsp	1 tsp	1 tsp

Peel, then quarter or slice the bananas and place on a piece of heavy-duty foil. Dot with butter or margarine and sprinkle with sugar and cinnamon. Wrap the fruit tightly in the foil.

Place on the barbecue 10–15 cm/4–6 inches above medium-hot coals. Cook for 6–8 minutes, turning the package over 2 or 3 times, until well heated through.

BARBECUED BANANAS WITH RUM Ⓥ

INGREDIENTS	Metric	Imperial	American
Large just-ripe bananas	4	4	4
Lemon juice	1 tbsp	1 tbsp	1 tbsp
Clear honey	2 tbsp	2 tbsp	2 tbsp
Light or dark rum	2 tbsp	2 tbsp	2 tbsp

Ahead of time, slit the banana skins down each side and remove half of each skin. Take the bananas out of the remaining half skins but keep the skins. Place the fruit in a shallow dish.

Warm the lemon juice and honey, mix in the rum and pour the mixture over the fruit. Leave for 15 minutes.

Replace the bananas in the half skins and place each, cut side up, on a piece of foil which will enclose it completely. Spoon any honey mixture in the dish over the fruit. Draw up the foil and twist it over the fruit.

Bake on the barbecue for about 15 minutes.

Note: Ginger wine is an excellent alternative to rum.

PINEAPPLE Ⓥ

INGREDIENTS	Metric	Imperial	American
Whole fresh pineapple	1	1	1
Clear honey	3–4 tbsp	3–4 tbsp	3–4 tbsp

Peel the pineapple, quarter it lengthways and remove the core. Then cut each quarter in half lengthways, giving you 8 spears. Place the spears on heavy-duty foil. Trickle the honey over them, then seal the packet tightly.

Place on the barbecue 10–15 cm/4–6 inches above hot or medium-hot coals. Cook, turning the package occasionally, for 8–10 minutes or until heated through.

Serve as a 'starter' at a midday barbecue or as a dessert.

ORANGES Ⓥ

INGREDIENTS	Metric	Imperial	American
Large oranges	3–4	3–4	3–4
Butter or margarine	1 tbsp	1 tbsp	1 tbsp
Sugar	1 tsp	1 tsp	1 tsp
Ground cinnamon	1 tsp	1 tsp	1 tsp

Peel the oranges, divide into segments and place on heavy-duty foil. Dot with the butter or margarine and sprinkle with the sugar and cinnamon.

Seal in the foil and place on the barbecue 10–15 cm/4–6 inches above hot or medium-hot coals. Cook, turning the package occasionally, for 6–8 minutes or until well heated through.

Serve as a dessert.

PEACHES Ⓥ

INGREDIENTS	Metric	Imperial	American
Medium-sized fresh peaches	4	4	4
Lemon juice	2 tsp	2 tsp	2 tsp
Butter or margarine	1 tbsp	1 tbsp	1 tbsp
Light brown sugar	2 tbsp	2 tbsp	2 tbsp

Peel the peaches and remove stones (pits). Slice and place on heavy-duty foil. Sprinkle with lemon juice, dot with butter or margarine and sprinkle with sugar.

Seal tightly in foil and place on the barbecue 10–15 cm/4–6 inches above hot or medium-hot coals. Cook, turning the packet several times, for 6–8 minutes or until well heated through.

Serve for dessert as a topping for ice-cream or sponge cake.

GINGER PEARS Ⓥ

INGREDIENTS	Metric	Imperial	American
Large dessert pears	2	2	2
Lemon juice for brushing			
Butter or margarine	4 tsp	4 tsp	4 tsp
Sugar	2 tsp	2 tsp	2 tsp
Ground ginger	2 tsp	2 tsp	2 tsp

Halve the pears lengthways and remove the cores with a teaspoon. Brush the cut sides with lemon juice.

Blend together the butter or margarine, sugar and ginger. Fill the core holes with the mixture and dot any remaining mixture over the pears.

Lay each half pear, cut side up, in the centre of a piece of foil which will enclose it. Draw up the edges of the foil and twist them together over the pears.

Place on the barbecue 10–15 cm/4–6 inches above medium-hot coals. Cook for about 10 minutes until well heated through.

Index